T0196042

DEFINING
Christianity

— IN BREVI —

BARBARA L. AYERS

WESTBOW
PRESS®
A DIVISION OF THOMAS NELSON
& ZONDERVAN

This book is a work of non-fiction. Unless otherwise noted, the author and the publisher make no explicit guarantees as to the accuracy of the information contained in this book and in some cases, names of people and places have been altered to protect their privacy.

WestBow Press books may be ordered through booksellers or by contacting:

WestBow Press
A Division of Thomas Nelson & Zondervan
1663 Liberty Drive
Bloomington, IN 47403
www.westbowpress.com
844-714-3454

Because of the dynamic nature of the Internet, any web addresses or links contained in this book may have changed since publication and may no longer be valid. The views expressed in this work are solely those of the author and do not necessarily reflect the views of the publisher, and the publisher hereby disclaims any responsibility for them.

Any people depicted in stock imagery provided by Getty Images are models, and such images are being used for illustrative purposes only.
Certain stock imagery © Getty Images.

Unless marked otherwise, all Scripture quotations are taken from The Holy Bible, New International Version®, NIV® Copyright © 1973, 1978, 1984, 2011 by Biblica, Inc.® Used by permission. All rights reserved worldwide.

Scripture quotations marked AMP are taken from the Amplified® Bible, Copyright © 2015 by The Lockman Foundation. Used by permission.

Scripture quotations marked MSG are taken from The Message. Copyright © 1993, 1994, 1995, 1996, 2000, 2001, 2002. Used by permission of NavPress Publishing Group.

Scripture quotations marked NLT are taken from the Holy Bible, New Living Translation, Copyright © 1996, 2004, 2015 by Tyndale House Foundation. Used by permission of Tyndale House Publishers, Inc., Carol Stream, Illinois 60188. All rights reserved.

ISBN: 978-1-6642-0482-9 (sc)
ISBN: 978-1-6642-0483-6 (hc)
ISBN: 978-1-6642-0481-2 (e)

Library of Congress Control Number: 2020916967

Print information available on the last page.

WestBow Press rev. date: 11/19/2020

To my grandsons, Nathan and Joseph.
May you always know
the love of God.
and live it.

To my father, Donald,
who always knew
the love of God.
and lived it.

A special thank you to my Christian teacher, supporter, and friend,
Carole LaJeunesse Harbour.
Carole, with her husband, Stan, and their family,
exemplify and radiate the Christian life.

Contents

A Defining Moment

ONCE UPON A time, I was a very shy, quiet child who preferred to remain in the background, watching everyone else go about their daily lives. This made it somewhat difficult for my inquisitive mind, always observing, studying, and analyzing everything around me, with few answers of my own that made any sense. My daddy was the one person I could go to for answers to my pervasive and internalized queries. I remember one time quite clearly—as though it were yesterday—although I was younger than ten at the time.

We had been talking about God and our beliefs. At one point, I asked Daddy what there was before God existed. My exact question was "What was before there was?" I remember his long, pondering pause while considering my ancient philosophical question. I can't help but wonder whether this classical philosophy professor was concerned or intrigued by this questioning from such a young mind. After all, it was not the typical sort of thing a ten-year-old would be considering. But he carefully went on to explain that the things of God are beyond our comprehension, even for grown-ups. And we must trust in God with something called *faith*.

Well, my daddy passed away shortly after, but my questioning never ceased. In fact, as I grew older and more studious, questions kept growing and propagating in my head. They became a part of so many of my studies and research papers over the decades. Yet it seemed the more I studied, the more questions I had about religion and people, the earthbound creatures and the spiritually unbound ones.

I knew I followed the Christian faith in my heart and mind the best I could with my limited understanding. But I found myself experiencing difficulties explaining my Christian beliefs to other people. The reality was that I was having trouble defining it clearly for myself. This is where I found myself floundering in life for many decades—very much as a deer in headlights when it came to defining Christianity and applying it to myself and my world.

I wanted to find answers and a way to understand and explain my beliefs. I required knowledge. I've discovered that the best learning modes for me are through reading and writing. So I began with widespread research parameters and resources. I scoured any book I could find on religion and philosophy. I read a lot and wrote copious notes. I took numerous classes and joined many study groups. I eventually discovered the best source for answers about Christianity came directly from studying the Word of God—the Bible. Although I may not have every answer secured at this point in my studies, I feel more confident in who I am and the life God desires for me and the world. And more importantly, I feel more comfortable in sharing what I now know for certain.

> Always be prepared to give an answer to everyone who asks you to give the reason for the hope that you have. But do this with gentleness and respect. (1 Pet. 3:15 NIV; see also Col. 4:5–6 NLT)

It is my hope and prayer this book will provide some of the answers you seek exactly as God intended—from his Word. I hope to serve as a guide through my own research into my faith. It is important to me that you begin to understand without being overwhelmed, so I've kept it short and focused on presenting what I feel are the ten essential areas to comprehending the basics of Christianity. This will not be an in-depth, theological analysis of Christianity. There are numerous books like that available. Furthermore, all the topic areas are much more interrelated with one another than what I will present herein. One cannot realistically discuss one without the others. However, I have attempted to keep each of them basic and on point for the sake of clarity.

I pray I am able to give you enough of what you need to push past any negative experiences you have had in life, and perhaps with religion itself. We all have those stories. I want to create a desire in you to move toward a knowledge that can be fantastically enlightening, encouraging, and exciting. Know that Christianity requires a lifetime of study and application, as does most anything in this earthly life. Great things take time.

I have always followed the philosophy that one cannot ever make the decision about religion (or many other things) without a foundation from which to pull knowledge. You simply cannot rationally decide about something if you have no solid knowledge base from which to begin. This is an indisputable fact. A fragmented understanding is not enough. With knowledge comes a depth of insight through an understanding and ability to discern the truth. God's truth is unshakable, whereas humankind's ever-changing truths fluctuate with the whims and fads of earthbound societal influences. Biology, behavior, and environment have been my favorite analytical tools in my discourses over the years. People influence one another tremendously in each of these areas. And every little once in a while, someone or something comes along to change the ebb and flow of reality as it is, only to become something else—for better or worse.

The reality is that human nature is flawed from the start. We have been given the freedom of choice, and we think we know it all. In the Bible, we have been given an instruction manual we refuse to read, because we think what we don't know we can figure out from trial and error. We are given a map with directions, but we think we know the way.

> The empty-headed treat life as a plaything; the perceptive grasp its meaning and make a go of it. Refuse good advice and watch your plans fail; take good counsel and watch them succeed. Congenial conversation—what a pleasure! The right word at the right time—beautiful! Life ascends to the heights for the thoughtful—it's a clean about-face from descent into hell. (Prov. 15:21–24 MSG)

None of us can deny the difficulties of making our way through this life on Earth. Each one of us has experiences unique and not so unique. We struggle at times. We all have stories. We all come from different places and perspectives. Some of us come from Christian backgrounds, while others do not. We are all searching for answers and something that makes sense and adds value to our lives. We experience life in different ways and are usually unsatisfied with how it is playing out. I offer you information and an opportunity to see things from a Christian perspective, although I am still learning myself. I am one of many on a journey to live life to the fullest. Take comfort in knowing you will never have to be on this journey alone.

It's time to educate and grow. You cannot cling to what was but rather need to jump into what is. Your maturity will transform your life into one of unity and peace—unity with God and peace with other people and yourself. I pray the clarity and certainty of these passages will become real by the time you read the last page.

> Listen to advice and accept discipline, and at the end you will be counted among the wise. Many are the plans in a person's heart, but it is the Lord's purpose that prevails. (Prov. 19:20–21 NIV)

God has a plan and purpose for each one of us. This is a fact in Christianity. Growing up, I always knew God was in my life plan. This was my first problem. I failed to understand I am supposed to fit into God's plan, not God into mine. Blindly, I did what so many people do. Christian or not, I fought for my own path and belief system. I thought I did not need any church to make my way through the great life I had planned. I didn't need any organized group or religion to work my way through life with my God. If only I knew then what I know now.

We must be surrounded by our Christian family. The purpose of the church is grounding by surrounding, so we can stop floundering. We all desperately need this in our lives. You will be amazed at how your life transforms when you surround yourself with God's loving family. Your heart is influenced by your surroundings, and your actions are illuminated by your heart. Love is the key to everything.

My first instinct is to defend my Christian beliefs through humankind's limited, concrete concepts. For example, I have always had a keen interest in biblical archeology and biological adaptation, and I followed these interests at university. Throughout the years when people heard this, I was barraged with arguments about how science does not validate or support the Bible.

"Well, it does," tended to flow from my mouth immediately. Without pause, I would push onward to argue, "Scientific advances and historical discoveries continuously present supporting, concrete facts of what we already find in the biblical record."

I have since come to know that science and its discoveries are constantly changing. Theories developed and presented in every scientific discipline come and go with every decade or less. The reality is this: creation is evidence enough. And God is enduring and unchanging.

> For since the creation of the world God's invisible qualities—his eternal power and divine nature—have been clearly seen, being understood from what has been made, so that people are without excuse. (Rom. 1:20 NIV)

5

Unfortunately, in my youth, I failed to grasp the most important thing. What is at the crux of this argument is really religion versus relationship—what you do versus what God has done, what is physical and earthly versus that which is spiritual and heavenly. Christianity is not about presenting physical proof of God or his plans for all humankind, which has existed since before creation. When you begin to understand this, the experience of God within you will ignite and expand, and faith will become enough. You will begin your journey of understanding, and an evolution of your heart will take place to create a trust in him. You have been called to experience the ever-revealing and unfolding mysteries of Christianity.

> I urge you to live a life worthy of the calling you have received. Be completely humble and gentle; be patient, bearing with one another in love. Make every effort to keep the unity of the Spirit through the bond of peace. There is one body and one Spirit, just as you were called to one hope when you were called; one Lord, one faith, one baptism; one God and Father of all, who is over all and through all and in all. (Eph. 4:1–6 NIV)

Ultimately, we all need saving. Saving from ourselves. Saving from earthly woes, entrapments, and sins. And especially saving from an eternity of punishment caused by our unrighteousness and estrangement from God. The only thing that can save us is trusting in God's Son, Jesus, and the message he brings from God. Simply explained, Jesus came into the world to atone for our sins and restore our relationship with God. Through the events chronicled in the Bible, we learn that our debts are paid for every bad choice we've ever made, and, as such, every one of us has the opportunity to experience salvation and eternal life through trust in Jesus.

We cannot reunite with God, live a rewarding life, and be saved from eternal death all by ourselves. It is through the grace of God, his free gift, that we have the opportunity. It is freely offered, and we are free to accept it or not. Know this: it is at that wondrous moment of acceptance we become filled with the Holy Spirit and the power of God. With this, we begin to learn of the mysteries of all that surrounds us.

> This is God's Message, the God who made the earth, made it livable and lasting, known everywhere as God: "Call to me and I will answer you. I'll tell you marvelous and wondrous things that you could never figure out on your own." (Jer. 33:3 MSG)

Acceptance of God's gift is a guarantee of an everlasting life of fulfillment. I have never been happier than when I acknowledged this and finally began to live a life guided by the Word of God. It does not make me perfect or my life flawless but continually guides me toward a more satisfying and enriching life. My relationships with God and other people have become so much more rewarding (see Mic. 6:8 MSG).

We are born physically dying, to which any biologist will attest. Therefore, shouldn't we attempt to live this life on earth to the fullest? And shouldn't we develop the spiritual lives we are gifted? I hope and pray that you will find something here. I want God to use me so you can find all he freely offers to you.

> [God] made known to us the mystery of his will according to his good pleasure, which he purposed in Christ, to be put into effect when the times reach their fulfillment—to bring unity to all things in heaven and on earth under Christ. (Eph. 1:9–10 NIV)

Tempus est de essentia.

God

"WHO, WHAT, WHERE, when, and why is God?" we earthbound mortals ask. In our search for answers, we are forced to accept that humankind cannot begin to grasp the nature or being of God. We are constrained by our earthly thoughts and understanding of everything. It is usually a disaster for us to attempt to define God, his actions, or even heaven based upon our limited frame of reference. We must rely on what God himself tells us.

GOD'S NAME, NATURE, AND CHARACTER

Let's begin with his name. God is referred to by many names in the Bible. I will discuss only a few of these here. You might enjoy looking into some more of these later. I also encourage you to look up the referenced Bible passages you will encounter in your reading to gain additional insights.

It is directly from God we learn the name by which he is to be called. In the Hebrew Bible, we find many different names for God. For example, "Yahweh" is a biblical name for God that means "I am." This comes from the verb "to be" and refers to the eternal existence of God as having no beginning or end. Indeed, this is stated by God when he calls himself the "Alpha and the Omega," the "First and the Last," and the "Beginning and the End." He is all these names, which are clear descriptors of the quality of his existence (see Rev. 1:8; Rev. 22:13; Exod. 3:14–15; and Isa. 43:11a MSG).

"Yahweh" along with the Hebrew names "Jehovah" and "Adonai" have been replaced in many biblical translations with "Lord," which is the Greek word for "master." Or sometimes they are replaced with "God," which is the Greek word *theos* commonly translated as "deity." The name "El Shaddai" from the Hebrew Bible means "the Almighty" (see Amos 4:13). As there are many different translations of the Bible, one can also find different terms that refer to God and the characteristics of God. But understand all translations maintain the same facts about him.

God is "spirit," as stated in John 4:24. From this, we know God is omniscient, having infinite and complete awareness, understanding, insight, and knowledge. He has full knowledge of everything. There is nothing God or "El Roi"—the God who sees me—doesn't know. He is aware of everything occurring everywhere. He understands everything we think, say, and do—even before we think, say, or do it. He has insight into our character and of what we are capable. He knows us completely, inside and out (see Ps. 139:1–6 AMP).

God is omnipresent, constant, and present everywhere at the same time. God is not bound by time or place. He has existed everywhere since before creation. Our conceptions of time and place are earthbound and finite, whereas God's are eternal and infinite. *Eternal* means something exists outside of, and is unaffected by, time. We know God is omnipresent, existing outside of time. Again we are reminded of the alpha and the omega of his existence. He exists everywhere at once and never goes away or gets winded as we do. He is forever unchanging (see James 1:17; Jer. 23:24; Isa. 40:28 MSG; and 2 Pet. 3:8).

In many of my group gatherings, I was frequently involved in discussions concerning not only the plausibility of God's creation of the world but that he did it within a mere seven days. We are always stuck thinking in terms of our own conception of time and concrete position within it. We tend to deny that which we cannot see or understand. As mere mortals, we can barely begin to imagine the planning process and the timing in human terms that would have to be undertaken for such a monumental feat to be drawn out and exacted. Our thoughts are earthbound. Fanciful speculation is all any of us is able to accomplish. The ultimate answers are out of our limited reach and understanding. But they are not for God—the omniscient and omnipotent Creator of all there is and will be (see 1 Chron. 29:11; Ps. 90:2, 4; and Matt. 19:26b).

God is unfathomable, beyond what any of us are capable of understanding. It is always amazing, stunning, thrilling, and somewhat intimidating when you come to realize God has made something mysterious and profound happen around you or to you. This aha moment can be both uncanny and exhilarating. But what can we truly know or understand about God? He is a mystery to us (see Job 11:7–8).

> "My thoughts are not your thoughts neither are your ways
> my ways," declares the Lord. "As the heavens are higher
> than the earth, so are my ways higher than your ways and
> my thoughts than your thoughts." (Isa. 55:8–9)

The power of God or "Elohim" is not restricted by humankind's limitations, physical or intellectual. Old women bear children, the sick and dying are healed, and the dead rise upon his command. I refer you to the stories of Elizabeth (see Luke 1:5–25), Sarah (see Gen. 18:1–14, 17:17), and Lazarus (see John 11:1–45) as just a few of the demonstrations of God's amazing omnipotence. It is through such examples we are taught not only of God's unlimited power but also to persevere and trust in God's plan. We cannot change or deny what God has planned since before creation. We see what he has done. We can't begin to imagine what he will do (see Job 42:2 and Ps. 139:7–10).

For ever since the world was created, people have seen the earth and sky. Through everything God made, they can clearly see his invisible qualities—his eternal power and divine nature. So they have no excuse for not knowing God. (Rom. 1:20 NLT; see also Ps. 19:1–4)

King David, a mortal man with both major faults and extreme faith, explicitly tells us who God is throughout his book of Psalms. We can feel the intense emotions in his rhapsody and see his world through the vivid descriptions of what God means to him. He praises God as his provider, refuge, savior, divine deliverer, shield, fortress, rock, redeemer, and his Lord, among other majestic things. You should read particularly Psalm 18.

God is always with us as our protector and savior. He loves us so very much and never hesitates to show or remind us. Unfortunately, most of the time, we forget to pay attention, because we are self-absorbed and focused on the worldly things around us. Just know that God is always there for each one of us. He will never abandon us. He loves us deeply and dearly (see Isa. 43:1–4 MSG).

God's character is revealed by his actions. He is both just and benevolent at the same time. He doesn't hesitate to punish or reward as he deems necessary. Throughout the Bible, we are shown examples of God's actions as creator, provider, deliverer, and an omnipotent Lord of all. God's actions always follow his plans, in his time, and in his ways.

He has made everything beautiful in its time. He has also set eternity in the human heart; yet no one can fathom what God has done from beginning to end. I know that there is nothing better for people than to be happy and to do good while they live. That each of them may eat and drink, and find satisfaction in all their toil—this is the gift of God. I know that everything God does will endure forever; nothing can be added to it and nothing taken from it. God does it so that people will fear him. (Eccles. 3:11–14)

It's always a good idea to look up the meaning of words in anything you read, even if they seem familiar to you. You will be amazed by what you find. For example, we often read that God has great mercy and loving-kindness for those who fear him. "Fear" is often translated in the Bible as reverence and respect, not as an unpleasant, emotional distress.

Our God is a jealous god. Once again, we need to look up the full meaning of this word. The jealousy of God has to do with how God behaves toward us as a loving father. He has an attitude of being covetous, desirous, protective, mindful, and intolerant of unfaithfulness (see Exod. 20:5, 34:14; Deut. 4:24, 5:9, 6:15, 32:16, 32:21; Josh. 24:19; Ezek. 36:5–6, 39:25; Nah. 1:2; Exod. 20:3 NLT; and Isa. 46:9).

There are no other gods. We are called to never worship idols or earthly things but to worship God first and only. We are expected to focus and prioritize him in our lives, for he is the first, last, and only God there is (see Isa. 44:6–8 MSG and Isa. 43:10b).

Treat God as holy, for he is indeed holy. *Merriam-Webster* defines *holy* as one who is "exalted or worthy of complete devotion as one perfect in goodness and righteousness." Treat God as trustworthy. He promises hope and salvation to those who trust in him and faithfully obey his holy law of love. God is our lifeline in this world and the next.

> Now when people take an oath, they call on someone greater than themselves to hold them to it. And without any question that oath is binding. God also bound himself with an oath, so that those who received the promise could be perfectly sure that he would never change his mind. So God has given both his promise and his oath. These two things are unchangeable because it is impossible for God to lie. Therefore, we who have fled to him for refuge can have great confidence as we hold to the hope that lies before us. This hope is a strong and trustworthy anchor for our souls. It leads us through the curtain into God's inner sanctuary. (Heb. 6:16–19 NLT)

So who is God to us, and why does he exist for us? In the next pages, we will begin to learn more about our God. But for now, know that God is loving, compassionate, faithful, giving, forgiving, and patient. But he will not hesitate to discipline or punish (see Exod. 34:6–7).

OUR HEAVENLY FATHER

Abba is an intimate name used by Jesus for *father*. God is the father of all. God loves all humankind and cares for us truly and deeply, as a parent for a child. We are his children, his precious children. We belong to the family of God (see John 1:12–13).

God the Father is the head of our Christian family. He is in charge of everything. We often forget this when we move through our daily lives. It is important to keep our focus on the instructions and directions of God as the leader of our household (see Eph. 4:6).

As a good father, God will teach, discipline, and reward his children. This is expected and necessary, even if it can be unpleasant at times. A good parent disciplines out of love for a child. We all have seen undisciplined children in public places and wonder where their parents have fled. All of us understand and appreciate a well-mannered child and a well-cultivated adult. They tend to reap the greatest rewards. Goodness naturally gravitates toward goodness. So understand God disciplines out of love and a desire for us to be just and righteous individuals (see Heb. 12:5–7a, 10b–11).

Young children often show anger and resentment when disciplined. But, as a good parent, God is not nearly as concerned with our happiness as he is with our holiness. He does indeed care for the future of his children. He wants to encourage us through his fatherly love (see Prov. 3:11–12).

God is omniscient and aware that we often make mistakes and commit sins. Yet he chooses to intervene for us as our Father. He does not dwell on our past but rather looks to our present for a better future. His purpose is to guide us to a more righteous way of being, a more satisfying way of existing with others. He looks to our survival (see Isa. 43:25 MSG and Ps. 130:3 NLT).

Yes, God does have specific rules he sets for us, his children. They are all based upon love. Loving God. Loving self. Loving others. Following his rule of love will guide us toward righteous living among one another. It gives us direction and is rewarding in the end (see Isa. 48:17).

God is our all-knowing parent, and we must obey him. We must not obey anyone or anything contrary to what is justifiable and morally right. Therefore, we can always trust in God's incorruptible Word to teach and guide us in the right way to go in life (see Matt. 15:1–6 NLT). We know we can count on God. We know he is a parent who takes good care of his children. We know God loves us and created everything for us. We know we live for him *and* because of him (see 1 Cor. 8:6a).

The Trinity

God is one being comprised of three distinct persons: the Father, the Son, and the Holy Spirit. Although the word *trinity* does not appear anywhere in scripture, it is commonly held that there are three divine elements or natures to the Godhead. Both the Old and New Testament scriptures contain inferences of three distinct persons yet one Godhead. This doctrine was largely formulated and the term in use by the fourth century AD.

God is sometimes referred to as the three-in-one. This is made up of God the Father, who gives us our identity as a family of grace; the Holy Spirit, who enlightens and empowers; and Jesus Christ, who dwells in our hearts through faith, as the source of transforming love. We are commanded to be baptized in the name of all three (see Eph. 3:14–17 and Matt. 28:19).

All three parts of the Godhead existed before creation. All three were involved in the creation of everything. All three are always present and involved in our lives. And all three will exist throughout eternity (see Gen. 1:26, 3:22, 11:7 and Isa. 6:8a).

God is our Creator with a plan, a purpose. God chose to reconcile with humankind by coming to earth in human form as Jesus Christ, who we call the Son of God. Because humans cannot understand the mysterious things of God, we require the Holy Spirit for discernment and knowledge of the faith and trust found through Jesus Christ. The Holy Spirit became available to us when Jesus ascended into heaven. We will explore these topics more in later chapters.

GOD'S ELECT OR CHOSEN

God's *elect* are individuals who were chosen, predestined for salvation before the creation. It is based upon God's choice, his plan, and *not* on any merit or acts foreseen in any individual. Through God's omniscience, the chosen are known to God and chosen to live holy lives worthy of his calling and grace (see Eph. 1:4–6 and 2 Tim. 1:9).

There are many thoughts on this topic of God's chosen. Most I have studied have to do with defining who is in control. In whom does responsibility and accountability lie? I have had a disagreement with various schools of thought on this subject. My belief is that control is not the issue, because God is ultimately in control of all. Rather, it is the consideration of the glorification of God through the defining attributes or characteristics, which he gave to humans at creation, that is the point. At some juncture in your Christian journey, you will want to decide what it is you choose to believe in this area. For now, I will share with you my current conclusions in two parts.

First, let's consider mortal humans. As humans were created in the image of God, we reflect his nature. We have free will just like the one who created us. God gave us free will in order for us to be able to make our own choice to obey or disobey his Word. We become mere programmed robots if we are not allowed to freely choose to act or not in accordance with the Word of God (see John 7:16–17 and Deut. 30:19–20).

We have some control over our destiny—but not ultimate control. I hold that most of us are able to hear the message of the Lord's salvation, if and when it is offered. And therefore, we must pay careful attention to what we are taught, so we do not drift away or ignore it in apathy (lack of responsiveness) or defy or attack it in apostasy (abandonment or rebellion). God wants everyone to be saved. His plan is to offer salvation to all people. It is up to each one of us to choose to accept or decline his free gift (see Heb. 2:1–3 NLT and 1 Tim. 2:1–4).

Second, God is ultimately in control of the minds and hearts of humankind. God may choose and guide a person in faithful obedience, softening their heart and removing the veil of ignorance, with the help of sanctification by the Holy Spirit. This is the process of changing a person's character to be used for God's intended purpose. Conversely, God may choose to keep a person ignorant and to harden their heart. They then cannot respond to God's calling to salvation (see Isa. 65:1; Prov. 16:9; and 1 Pet. 1:1–2).

My conclusion is that God softens and opens the hearts of the elect when he chooses to call to them. Those who are called have the God-given freedom of choice to hear the messages that Jesus brings. They are never forced or coerced into doing so. There are times, though, when God chooses to harden a heart and places a veil of ignorance so they cannot hear the call. This is his choice, according to his plan. Beyond this, it is totally up to us to use those attributes God purposefully chose to bestow upon us, to respond in faithful obedience or not. Our choice at his request or calling. It is in *this act* of acceptance we give glory to God (see Rom. 9:16–23 NLT and John 12:38–40 NLT).

Jesus's parable of the farmer who planted his seed is a great example of our potential destinies that were set in motion before creation. Jesus spreads the Word of God, which is the seed. And the various effects on the plant's growth depend on the receptivity of a person's heart, which is the soil. A person responds to God's Word based upon the condition of their heart. It is my belief that both God and humans have the ability to choose whether to harden or soften the heart, to amend the soil by adding nutrients. However, it is God who will make the ultimate decision (see Luke 8:4–15 NLT; Matt. 13:3b–9 NLT; and Mark 4:14–20 MSG).

RECONCILIATION

God sent us his Son to bridge the chasm in our relationship created by the fall of Adam. This first man was given the freedom of choice. Sadly, his choice to disobey God and follow his own selfish desires led to his expulsion from the garden of Eden and resulted in a broken relationship with God. Now God knew this would happen and had made plans for it long before creation.

God desires to reunite and have a personal relationship with each one of us, so much so that he sacrificed his own Son for this relationship. You see, God cannot have anything to do with sin, and all sins must be punished. So Jesus came and took our sins upon himself, suffering tremendous and vicious atrocities and dying on the cross in our place. He took our punishment to atone for our sins so we could once again have a close relationship with God (see Acts 17:27 NLT and Jer. 29:13).

God will seek out each one of us to the ends of the earth to reconcile. This is how much he wants to have a personal relationship with us. He desires to reunite us with his loving family. A huge price was paid to restore these relationships. The plan is to make things right again (see Isa. 43:7).

Don't ever forget, God surpasses all humankind's comprehension and understanding. The things of God are a mystery to mortal humans. God is huge. Yet even so, God desires and works out opportunities to have a relationship with us. It is our own choice to accept or decline his calling.

> This is what the Lord says, he who made the earth, the Lord who formed it and established it—the Lord is his name: "Call to me and I will answer you and tell you great and unsearchable things you do not know." (Jer. 33:2–3; see also Rev. 3:20a)

God knows our hearts. God knows all. We can't ever hide from God. Our hearts, minds, and bodies are known to him. We are to have an intimacy in our personal relationship with God. He seeks to reward us in our close relationship with him. It is only possible to know God in his own chosen times and ways. So seek him out always. Open the door to your heart and invite him in. The rewards are truly great (see Ps. 37:4 and Matt. 6:33).

God's Plan

God gives humankind a freedom of choice in thought and action. We must understand that with this freedom brings the end results or consequences for each of the choices we make. These choices define our humanity as individuals, groups, and as a whole. So we must act responsibly, with righteousness in our hearts and exhibited in our thoughts and actions.

Also know that God has a freedom of choice. The difference is God has a purpose, a plan that has existed since before creation—before our time began. The history of God proves he has always had a plan. We were created for God's glory, as part of his plan. We must fit into God's plan, not God's plan into our lives (see 1 Cor. 2:7 and Acts 17:26 NLT).

We can look gladly to God's ultimate plans for humankind, for it is a perfect plan. He designed it totally for us. We must be patient at times. The rewards for our trust in and faithfulness to him will be grand (see Isa. 30:18 MSG)!

God is clear his plan is to have an eternal, loving relationship with us. Those who refuse or deny him will reap their just rewards. God is faithful, loves us unfailingly, and keeps his promises. We must be obedient and do the same. Consequences always follow actions. Weigh your thoughts and actions carefully. For as much as God delights in rewarding our good behavior, he will not hesitate to punish our bad.

> The one sitting on the throne said, "Look, I am making everything new!" And then he said to me, "Write this down, for what I tell you is trustworthy and true." And he also said, "It is finished! I am the Alpha and the Omega— the Beginning and the End. To all who are thirsty I will give freely from the springs of the water of life. All who are victorious will inherit all these blessings, and I will be their God, and they will be my children."

> "But cowards, unbelievers, the corrupt, murderers, the immoral, those who practice witchcraft, idol worshipers, and all liars—their fate is in the fiery lake of burning sulfur. This is the second death." (Rev. 21:5–8 NLT; see also Deut. 7:9–10 NLT)

God does have an ultimate purpose. Everything happens as he wills it. But you are not on your own. Don't think that God does not hear our petitions and prayers. He does indeed hear us. God hears our voices, whether in joyful praise or silent pleading. He has an intimate knowledge of us. Maintain an everlasting faith in him to always be with you.

God is like oxygen. You can't see him, but you need him to survive. He is always available to you. Just ask (see Luke 12:36).

We cannot ascribe human qualities to God. God is not human. God does not speak and then not act. God does not promise and then not fulfill (see Num. 23:19). We can always depend on God and his Word. We can trust God. God expects our faithful obedience as his children. He offers us salvation and a renewed, refreshing relationship with him (see Isa. 45:22–23a NLT).

Jesus tells us the key to God's eternal plan:

Very truly I tell you, whoever hears my word and believes him who sent me has eternal life and will not be judged but has crossed over from death to life. Very truly I tell you, a time is coming and has now come when the dead will hear the voice of the Son of God and those who hear will live. (John 5:24–25; see also John 6:29)

Jesus Christ

JESUS HAS ALWAYS existed, even before the beginning of creation. He became flesh and lived among us on earth to testify to the truth and to reconcile us to God. It is in this truth that we learn about all that has to do with reality and existence and the very essence and being of God—the who, what, where, why, and how of God and all that exists. Ultimately, an encounter with Jesus leads to a revelation of God (see 1 Tim. 2:5–6 NLT).

> Jesus is the exact representation of God's being. He is God incarnate. Jesus is indeed fully God and fully man. Through him, the mysteries of God are revealed (see John 1:18 NLT).

> Jesus was involved in creation. All things were created through him. He is the divine Word. Jesus sustains everything by his powerful Word (see John 1:1–3, 14; John 18:37; Heb. 1:3; 1 Cor. 8:6; Col. 1:16; and John 10:28–30 AMP).

Jesus often refers to himself as God did, "I am" (see John 8:58). As we look further into the book of John in the Bible, we can see all the descriptors used for who Jesus is, where he is from, and what his purpose is here on earth. All these are found in the many declarations of himself in "I am."

- In John 6:35, 41, 48, and 51, Jesus refers to himself as "the bread of life" "that came down from Heaven," to give eternal life.
- In John 8:23, Jesus declares, "I am from above. I am not from this world."
- John 8:12 and 9:5 tell us Jesus informs the people he is "the light of the world." So no one will ever "walk in darkness."
- John 10:7–14 begins the "I am" discourses of Jesus as the gate or door for "the sheep" and "the good shepherd" "who lays down his life for his sheep."
- John 11:25–26 is clear about Jesus's purpose here on earth: "I am the resurrection and the life." And whoever believes in him will have eternal life.
- John 14:6 also very clearly states his purpose, "I am the way and the truth and the life." We can reach God, obtain knowledge of the truth, and gain eternal life only through Jesus.
- John 13:13 states Jesus is our "Lord" and "teacher."
- John 15:1–5 describes Jesus as "the vine," and it's through him that we become productive, fruitful people on this earth.

The Great I Am chose to live among humankind, to share in our humanity, in order to restore a personal relationship with us. This had been damaged by Adam's original sin. Jesus came to repair or harmonize our relationship with God, which began with the fall of Adam. God came in the human form of Jesus to reconcile us with himself, to change our estranged relationship. Jesus became the great mediator between humans and God.

Jesus came for our sanctification, to make us holy. He has shown us a way to become holy in fulfilling God's purpose for us to become a righteous people, to learn how to behave as morally just people. Alas, there was a heavy price to pay. An atonement or sacrifice was required for our offenses. Jesus gave himself as that sacrifice to redeem us, to pay the fine in order to bring us back to God. Jesus came for the purification of our sins. He has cleansed us with his sacrificial blood.

*E*XACTING ANCIENT PROPHECY

We can look to the Old Testament scriptures to understand that the life, ministry, and death of Jesus had been foretold for centuries prior to his appearance. Many of the facts concerning the life and divine purpose of Jesus were detailed with astonishing accuracy. The details are uncanny to us simpleminded mortal people. Yet, it was a well-established belief among the people in biblical lands that a savior or messiah would be coming into the world.

Many people in Jesus's day wanted God to come in a blaze of fire and calculated triumph, much like a warrior who has come to conquer. Their hearts were full of vengeance and greed. It is the characteristics of a person's heart that are crucial to any possible understanding of the divine purpose of Jesus Christ.

Jesus had to come as a tiny baby—to grow up in the world and to experience what we experience—in order to be able to say he was genuinely able to commiserate with us and that he was qualified to lead us. All this was the plan in order to be able to save us and to reconcile us to God. Many people back then were blinded and lacked a deeper understanding. Even today, we see this lack of comprehension for why Jesus had to arrive the way he did (see John 12:37–41).

Jesus was both denied and scorned. Even among the religious leaders, he was believed yet rejected and despised (see Isa. 53:3 and John 12:42–43). Jesus reminds us his rejection was the fulfillment of Old Testament prophecy (see John 15:25 NLT). People either refuted or ignored the prophecies. The veil of ignorance was over their eyes. People preferred to accept only the unchanging, earthly things that were congruent with their own beliefs and daily lives. They still do today, for the most part.

The purpose of Jesus on earth was clearly stated long before his arrival. He was to bring forth justice and righteousness for humankind. It was not to come as an act of war or violence but rather as a mission of peace. He brought divine order with his presence (see Zech. 9:9-10).

> Here is my servant, whom I uphold, my chosen one in whom I delight; I will put my Spirit on him, and he will bring justice to the nations. He will not shout or cry out, or raise his voice in the streets. A bruised reed he will not break, and a smoldering wick he will not snuff out. In faithfulness he will bring forth justice; he will not falter or be discouraged till he establishes justice on earth. In his teaching the islands will put their hope.
>
> I, the Lord, have called you in righteousness; I will take hold of your hand. I will keep you and will make you to be a covenant for the people and a light for the Gentiles, to open eyes that are blind, to free captives from prison and to release from the dungeon those who sit in darkness.
>
> See, the former things have taken place, and new things I declare; before they spring into being I announce them to you. (Isa. 42:1–4, 6–7, 9)

The prophet Isaiah lived *seven hundred years before* the birth of Jesus. Most people have heard the prophecy that Jesus would be born of a virgin from the house of David. The Hebrew name Immanuel, declared in Isaiah, means "God with us." Jesus is God come down to earth in human form to be with us. Living among us, Jesus would be directing us in choosing the right and rejecting the wrong (see Isa. 7:13–16 and Jer. 23:5).

In quite stunning detail, Isaiah describes the life and death of Jesus. As a sheep to the slaughter, the Lamb of God was to become sin for our sins. God would send his Son to take our cruel and brutal punishment upon himself, all this in order to become our blessed source of salvation. The ultimate goal was for all of us to be reconciled to God.

> Who has believed our message and to whom has the arm of the Lord been revealed? He grew up before him like a tender shoot, and like a root out of dry ground. He had no beauty or majesty to attract us to him, nothing in his appearance that we should desire him. He was despised and rejected by mankind, a man of suffering, and familiar with pain. Like one from whom people hide their faces he was despised, and we held him in low esteem.

> Surely he took up our pain and bore our suffering, yet we considered him punished by God, stricken by him, and afflicted. But he was pierced for our transgressions, he was crushed for our iniquities; the punishment that brought us peace was on him, and by his wounds we are healed. We all, like sheep, have gone astray, each of us has turned to our own way; and the Lord has laid on him the iniquity of us all.

> He was oppressed and afflicted, yet he did not open his mouth; he was led like a lamb to the slaughter, and as a sheep before its shearers is silent, so he did not open his mouth. By oppression and judgment he was taken away. Yet who of his generation protested? For he was cut off from the land of the living; for the transgression of my people he was punished. He was assigned a grave with the wicked, and with the rich in his death, though he had done no violence, nor was any deceit in his mouth.

> Yet it was the Lord's will to crush him and cause him to suffer, and though the Lord makes his life an offering for sin, he will see his offspring and prolong his days, and the will of the Lord will prosper in his hand. After he

has suffered, he will see the light of life and be satisfied;
by his knowledge my righteous servant will justify many,
and he will bear their iniquities. Therefore I will give him
a portion among the great, and he will divide the spoils
with the strong, because he poured out his life unto death,
and was numbered with the transgressors. For he bore the
sin of many, and made intercession for the transgressors.
(Isa. 53:1–12; see also Ps. 22:1–31)

Even before the prophet Isaiah made these declarations concerning Jesus, we can read about the events surrounding a man called David. King David, the second king of Israel, was a faithful and obedient servant of God. He was a favorite of God and was richly blessed by him.

It was through him the family line of Jesus was established. David was assured that God's Son would walk among humankind, demonstrating good judgment and morally right actions, and establish an eternal kingdom on earth (see Isa. 11:1–5, 10–11 and Mic. 5:2–4).

Many other individuals we learn about through Old Testament scriptures are of the ancestral line leading to Jesus. This genealogical picture is laid out concisely in forty-two generations from Abraham to Joseph, the husband of Mary, who was the mother of Jesus. We can read this in its entirety in the very beginning of the book of the New Testament, Matthew 1:1–17.

Upon the death and resurrection of Jesus, the prophecies of Isaiah had been fulfilled. When he first appeared to them following his death, Jesus told his disciples prophecy would be fulfilled in God's plan—through his life, death, and resurrection (see Luke 24:44–46 and Luke 1:68–70).

St. Augustine said it concisely in his well-known axiom: "In the Old Testament the New Testament is concealed; in the New Testament the Old Testament is revealed."

*D*IVINE BIRTH—DIVINE PURPOSE

Jesus was conceived by the Spirit of God. All this was foretold and prophesized hundreds of years before. He was part of God's plan for our salvation and reconciliation (see Matt. 1:18–23 and Luke 1:26–35).

Because God's children are human beings, made of flesh and blood, his Son also became flesh and blood. He needed to show us that he could understand our lives and experiences firsthand. There would be no value or meaningful purpose otherwise. In becoming flesh, Jesus would be able to defeat death in the end. Jesus was and is the promise of God to humankind—past, present, and future (see Heb. 2:14).

Even as Jesus came into the world, which was made through him, it did not recognize or accept him. Yet, in spite of this rejection, he still came with a solid promise (see John 1:10–13). The promise of a new covenant, which God brings to us through Jesus, is important to the foundation of Christianity. It explains the divine purpose of Jesus here on earth. It outlines a plan to make God known to everyone and to make reconciliation with God possible (see Jer. 31:31–34).

Why did God send his Son to be among us? This is the key to Christianity! Jesus brings us the free gift of salvation and the promise of eternal life, which come to those who trust and believe in him as the Son of God. And we must do this faithfully and obediently.

> For God so loved the world that he gave his one and only Son, that whoever believes in him shall not perish but have eternal life. For God did not send his Son into the world to condemn the world, but to save the world through him. Whoever believes in him is not condemned, but whoever does not believe stands condemned already because they have not believed in the name of God's one and only Son. (John 3:16–18)

$\mathcal{T}$HE NAMES OF JESUS

The name Jesus means "to deliver or rescue," as in the meaning of the word *salvation,* and describes his role as Savior. Jesus is the Latin form of the Hebrew name Yeshua, or Greek Joshua, both meaning "Yahweh is salvation."

Christ comes from the Greek, meaning "anointed one." In Hebrew, it is equivalent to "Messiah." These two names Jesus discourage his disciples from using. He wanted to prevent excitement in the populace, to avoid politicizing him, which would bring with it deviating and undesirable expectations. It was difficult enough to spread his message without taking it into a different direction. There was a plan and a purpose, and they needed to stay on course (see Douglas 2011).

We find in both the Old and New Testaments that Jesus holds many titles as he establishes God's kingdom on earth (see Isa. 9:6–7). He is known by what he does for us. He has and still does act as our counselor, advocate, peacemaker, mediator, redeemer, savior, cornerstone, rock, light, bridegroom, author and perfecter of our faith, head of the church, Son of God, Lamb of God, lion of the tribe of Judah, and Lord of all. Just to name a few.

Considerable amounts of scripture are devoted to the discussion of Jesus as the light and the truth, the shepherd and the lamb, and the rock and the cornerstone. Let's look at these three a little closer.

Illumination by the Light and the Truth

Jesus is the light of God, both visible and hidden, sent to reveal to all of us the two different paths of life and death. Jesus is the light we need in a world full of darkness to find the path to life. He came to shine in the midst of our darkness, to keep us from wandering around blindly (see John 8:12 and John 1:4–5, 9). The purpose of Jesus being our light is to touch our hearts, to effect a change in our hearts. Our heart reveals our character and its level of motivation to participate in life. In fulfillment of God's plan, our changed hearts become illuminated by the light that continually fills us with the knowledge and truth given through Jesus (see 2 Cor. 4:6).

But some people are so afraid to let go of any control over their stifling, predictably routine lives. And they definitely don't want any light shining on the bad things in their life. They tend to focus on their own earthly wants and needs, at any cost, without ever considering the big picture and any participation in it. There is a weird comfort for them within the status quo of having chaos in their life. They hide from the truth and the light (see John 3:19–21 and John 17:17).

The truth offered to us is the reality of all there is. Jesus came to be our guide—to lead us out of the darkness and into the light and the best of parts of reality. Ignorance is never blissful. It is merely a void, an emptiness. We must come out of the vacuum of darkness and be open to learning about the truth surrounding us. We need to walk with one another in the knowledge of God's truth. Such joy and peace can be found in walking together in a shared Christian journey (see 1 John 1:7).

Cared for by the Shepherd and the Lamb

Jesus tells us not to be anxious for anything. As a shepherd does for his sheep or a parent does for his child, he provides for all our security and needs. Jesus is our shepherd who is always with us and guides us along the right path.

Jesus came into the world to save all of us, not just some or a few. Every single one of us is valued and loved by God. If one of us strays away from his group, he will come after them and return this beloved to his fold of other Christians. It is his desire to never lose a single one of us. The Good Shepherd leaves the ninety-nine to recover the lost one. He rejoices and celebrates in finding the lost ones. Every one of us is a highly valued member of God's family. Each one of us is just that important. It is the will of God none of us perish (see Matt. 18:12–14 NLT; Luke 15:3–7, John 10:11, 14–15; and Luke).

Jesus was God's perfect sacrificial lamb. God chose him to pay for our sins with his life. Our sins are washed away through the payment of his spilled blood. Sins of the past, the present, and the future are forgiven. He suffered God's wrath when he took upon himself all the sins of humankind. He was the lamb without blemish or fault who was slain in our place. He was sacrificed to pay for our sins. His body was battered and broken for us. He gives us life through his death. We trust and believe in him for what he has done for us (see 1 Pet. 1:18–21 and John 1:29, 36).

Built upon the Rock and the Cornerstone

Jesus is our rock. He is the spiritual rock that is the foundation of the church, which is the people of faith. There is a common error of misunderstanding in the use of the term *church*. It is often thought of strictly as a building or earthly structure. However, in the Bible, it usually refers to the true believers of Christ. It's the people, the followers of Jesus who are the church. Jesus is the solid foundation upon which we, the church, build our lives (see Matt. 7:24–25 MSG).

With Jesus as the chief cornerstone, believers join together to establish the church of God's people and to serve as the temples of the Holy Spirit. Each one of us, as building blocks, represent a dwelling in which the Holy Spirit resides. We become one building, one family in Jesus. He is our foundation and the cornerstone joining us all together. He gives us direction and reference for our lives (see Eph. 2:19–22 and Gal. 3:28).

Yes, Jesus is the stone who was rejected by humans and became the foundation for believers to become both protected and productive. He is the secure and reliable cornerstone of God's church in the new covenant relationship (see Matt. 21:42–44; Ps. 118:22; and Isa. 28:16–18).

ATONEMENT AND OBEDIENCE

The atonement on the cross fulfills the Old Testament covenant requirement of having a blood sacrifice. Christ was obedient to God and shed his blood, dying on the cross as payment for all our sins. Sins bring consequences and required punishments. Jesus takes upon himself the punishment for all our sins. Through his unselfish actions, we are able to understand faithful and righteous obedience to God (see Rom. 3:25).

Jesus knows the struggles of human beings. As a man, he can empathize with humankind's struggles. He has been rejected, falsely accused, betrayed, abandoned, humiliated, ridiculed, publicly scourged and brutalized, tortured, beaten, bloodied, and nailed to a cross until dead. Yet he never sinned. And he never gave up on God's plan for our salvation and reconciliation (see Heb. 4:15).

The sum total of all the world's iniquity hung on the cross with Jesus. He knew no sin but became sin so we could be forgiven and set free from the consequences of our sins (see 2 Cor. 5:21). As God cannot associate with sin, Jesus suffered and bore the sins of the world *alone* on the cross. And still he did not give up on us.

We are asked to have the same attitude Christ had. He gave up his divine privileges and became human. He humbled himself in obedience to God and died a tortured, criminal's death on the cross. He had a choice. He unselfishly chose to save us. Death has been conquered through his obedience to God (see Phil. 2:6–8 and John 10:17–18).

> Very truly I tell you, whoever hears my word and believes him who sent me has eternal life and will not be judged but has crossed over from death to life. Very truly I tell you, a time is coming and has now come when the dead will hear the voice of the Son of God and those who hear will live. For as the Father has life in himself, so he has granted the Son also to have life in himself. And he

has given him authority to judge because he is the Son of Man.

Do not be amazed at this, for a time is coming when all who are in their graves will hear his voice and come out—those who have done what is good will rise to live, and those who have done what is evil will rise to be condemned. By myself I can do nothing; I judge only as I hear, and my judgment is just, for I seek not to please myself but him who sent me. (John 5:24–30; see also Rom. 8:1–2)

DEATH AND RESURRECTION

The possibility of the resurrection of the dead was a long-standing, commonly held belief by the Jewish people at the time of Jesus. It is this belief that made Christianity feasible in that particular time and place. It did not seem so far-fetched that Jesus rose from the dead. It was an acceptable, tolerable belief.

God's plan came together flawlessly. I am not surprised but almost always awed by the whats and whens of God's plan. Jesus came to fulfill the prophecies and the promises of God found in Old Testament scriptures. He was to die for our sins and be resurrected to give us new life (see 1 Cor. 15:3–4). It occurred at the right time, at the right place, and in the right way. It's like watching what happens when we drop a stone into the water. The plop and backsplash. And then the outward thrusting ripples, forever extending their reach outward. We are now feeling the effects of that stone on the water.

Jesus foretold his own death and resurrection three times in New Testament scriptures. His apostles wrote about what Jesus had told them concerning the specifics of what would happen to him in the days leading to his death and resurrection. These things would be done in accordance with God's plan. All Jesus foretold came true. God's promises to us were fulfilled upon the cross (see Matt. 20:17–19; Mark 8:31–33; Mark 9:30–32; Mark 10:32–33; Luke 13:31–33; Luke 18:31–33; and John 2:16–22).

On the cross, Jesus said, "It is finished." There is great meaning in this last statement by Jesus. It meant the debt for our sins had been paid. This part of God's plan had been fulfilled (see John 19:28–30). We are justified and sanctified by the blood of Christ. Because of his death and resurrection, we are cleansed and given the opportunity to become righteous in the sight of God (see Rom. 4:25).

There were hundreds of people who witnessed the resurrected Jesus Christ. The apostles Peter, Luke, and Paul all wrote about the resurrection of Jesus (see Acts 10:39–43; Acts 1:3, 9–11; Luke 24:13–51; and 1 Cor. 15:3–8). Resurrection and ascension are fundamental to Christianity and God's plan. Through the resurrection of Jesus Christ, we can leave death behind and become alive in him. For as death came through the man Adam, so life does also through the man Jesus (see 1 Cor. 15:20–22 and Acts 4:12).

Salvation is made possible only through the resurrection of Jesus. And we can share in the death and resurrection when we die to self and come to life in Christ. The Bible calls it being "born again." We leave behind the death that comes from our sins and become alive from righteous living in Christ. We are renewed, refreshed, and motivated to become productive and fruitful members of society.

RECONCILIATION THROUGH LOVE AND REGAINING LIFE THROUGH FAITH

Jesus's ministry was one of reconciliation, of restoring relationships. It is through our Lord Jesus Christ we have established our faith and are reconciled with God. Everything God has done comes out of his love for us. We were terrible, sinful people. Yet he still loved us. The sacrifice of his Son as payment for our sins demonstrates his love, his desire to renew a relationship with us (see Rom. 5:8–11).

The apostle Paul writes often that we need to share in this genuine love shown by God. We are reunited with one another through the cross. We are all able to have access to God. And we can live in peace with one another, because of what we now know (see Eph. 2:14–18). Everyone is invited to share in the salvation and reconciliation offered through Jesus. We must become ambassadors for Jesus. We are expected to help spread the message of Jesus to the world (see 2 Cor. 5:18–20).

We can all rely on the new, loving relationship with God and one another received through the death and resurrection of Jesus. The apostle John describes our new relationships. These are relationships based upon love.

> This is how God showed his love among us: He sent his one and only Son into the world that we might live through him. This is love: not that we loved God, but that he loved us first and sent his Son as an atoning sacrifice for our sins.
>
> [The] Father has sent his Son to be the Savior of the world. If anyone acknowledges that Jesus is the Son of God, God lives in them and they in God. And so we know and rely on the love God has for us. God is love. Whoever lives in love lives in God, and God in them. (1 John 4:9–10, 14b–16)

Christ is the one and only way to approach God and to enter the kingdom of God. Your good works and honest deeds will never get you into heaven. This is clearly delineated in the scriptures (see John 14:6–7, 11:25–26, and 14:9–10). Only our faith in Christ can save us from death, which is the just punishment for our sins. He brings us the gift of freedom to experience a good, sin-free life on earth and an eternal life with him in heaven.

So, by faith, we are in Christ and Christ is in us. Christ lives in us. He transforms us through our unity with him. We become Christlike in heart, thought, and deed. We become one with the will of God. We become love personified (see John 14:19–20).

The purity of the Lamb of God has washed over us. Enjoy the experience of having a transformed heart of love (see Gal. 4:4–6). As a new creation in Jesus, we need to be alert to those who are oppressed or in need. We are called to emulate the love we have been shown. Be a good example in doing good things for yourself and for others. Love and service reveal that we are in the family of Jesus (see John 14:12 and Acts 10:38).

Jesus lived a life we can't—free of sin and full of heart. Jesus suffered a death we should have, as punishment for our sins. Yet Jesus offers a life we can have through him as a free gift. Accept this in the love in which it is offered.

> The Son is the image of the invisible God, the firstborn over all creation. For in him all things were created: things in heaven and on earth, visible and invisible, whether thrones or powers or rulers or authorities; all things have been created through him and for him. He is before all things, and in him all things hold together. And he is the head of the body, the church; he is the beginning and the firstborn from among the dead, so that in everything he might have the supremacy. For God was pleased to have all his fullness dwell in him, and through him to reconcile to himself all things, whether things on earth or things in heaven, by making peace through his blood, shed on the cross.
>
> Once you were alienated from God and were enemies in your minds because of your evil behavior. But now he has reconciled you by Christ's physical body through

death to present you holy in his sight, without blemish and free from accusation—if you continue in your faith, established and firm, and do not move from the hope held out in the gospel. (Col. 1:15–23)

Holy Spirit

THE SPIRIT OF God was present at the creation. It was the breath or wind that animated creation. It enters and awakens the spiritual life within each and every living creature (see Gen. 1:1–2 NLT; Ps. 33:6; and Job 26:13 NLT).

The Holy Spirit lives within every believer. Of this we are promised by God. He will fill our hearts with love and righteousness and serve as a guide to us throughout our time on earth. We can call on him at any time for anything.

> I will give you a new heart and put a new spirit in you; I will remove from you your heart of stone and give you a heart of flesh. And I will put my Spirit in you and move you to follow my decrees and be careful to keep my laws. (Ezek. 36:26–27; see also Rom. 5:5)

While grace comes from Jesus Christ, love comes from God, and fellowship comes from the Holy Spirit. He is one of the best friends one could ever have. The Holy Spirit is within us to guide us into righteous living and a relationship with God and one another (see 2 Cor. 13:14).

$\mathcal{T}$HE GIFT

The Holy Spirit is given to all those who wholeheartedly ask (see 1 Thess. 1:5 and Acts 10:44). It is the character of the heart that determines who will receive the Holy Spirit. God does not hold back his gift of the Holy Spirit from anyone who asks with an open heart—a repentant heart. We must believe with faithful obedience to receive this blessed gift (see Luke 11:13 and Acts 15:8).

The power of the Holy Spirit comes on all who truly desire to hear the gospel message. Obedient confession of our sins and genuine repentance allows us to receive the Holy Spirit. It's that simple. God gives the Spirit without measure. We are all equal, no matter the sins, once we confess and repent (see Acts 2:38 and John 3:34).

My greatest thrill was being baptized in the Jordan River a few years ago. An inner strength and confidence truly burgeoned in this once shy, quiet person on that day. It has not made me perfect but has definitely changed my awareness of my thoughts and actions in the world around me. I would highly recommend a baptism or rebaptism, not for a proclamation to the world necessarily but more for encouragement to yourself. A repurposing of your life. What begins inside of you will blossom. Feel the gift of the Holy Spirit fill your life.

> As soon as Jesus was baptized, he went up out of the water. At that moment heaven was opened, and he saw the Spirit of God descending like a dove and alighting on him. (Matt. 3:16)

In the Old Testament, the book of Joel takes place during the days of Pentecost, which was a seven-day harvest festival celebrating the gift of the Ten Commandments to Moses. In Joel, God makes a promise to fill us with the powers of the Holy Spirit (see Joel 2:28–29). In the New Testament, Pentecost transformed to become a festival to commemorate the Holy Spirit descending upon the apostles. We too can celebrate the Holy Spirit descending upon us as promised.

Peter explains the powers witnessed in some people do not come from human origin but rather are divinely inspired by God through the Holy Spirit. God fills us with the Holy Spirit, who illuminates, guides, and transforms us in unique and significant ways as we become obedient to him (see 2 Pet. 1:20–21).

*D*IVINE ILLUMINATOR

The Holy Spirit is the divine illuminator—the giver of enlightenment, which is the knowledge of all things. He lifts the veil of ignorance and gives both insights and inspiration (see 2 Cor. 3:13–18). We could never discover the mysteries of God or the benefits of Christ's death by ourselves (see 1 Cor. 2:7). The Spirit of God is the Holy Spirit living within every believer as a guide to understanding God's plan and purpose.

> No one has ever seen God; but if we love one another, God lives in us and his love is made complete in us.
>
> This is how we know that we live in him and he in us: He has given us of his Spirit. And we have seen and testify that the Father has sent his Son to be the Savior of the world. If anyone acknowledges that Jesus is the Son of God, God lives in them and they in God. (1 John 4:12–15)

We are given the Holy Spirit as a source of wisdom and revelation. Through the Holy Spirit, we will come to know God (see Eph. 1:17 and 2 Tim. 1:14). God desires each one of us to know him and to understand his plan and purpose. The Holy Spirit gives us insights into the mind and heart of God. We cannot begin to comprehend the mind of God by ourselves. This spiritual understanding can only come with discernment from the Holy Spirit.

$\mathcal{A}$DVOCATE AND TEACHER

After his ascension into heaven, Jesus assures us we will never be alone. The Holy Spirit will be an advocate within each of us to support and advise us as we navigate through this world (see John 15:26 NLT).

We are given the Spirit of Truth, the Holy Spirit, to guide us in the comprehension of the Word of God (see John 14:16–17 and John 16:13–15). The Holy Spirit helps us to learn and follow the truths of the gospel message.

Only the Holy Spirit can discern the truths of God. Humans cannot begin to understand the spiritual realities. Illumination and revelation come only by the Holy Spirit. The unenlightened person does not have the Spirit of God or the mind of Christ. This contrasts with the Christian who does. The veil of ignorance can only be removed by the Holy Spirit.

> As it is written: "What no eye has seen, what no ear has heard, and what no human mind has conceived"—the things God has prepared for those who love him—these are the things God has revealed to us by his Spirit.
>
> The Spirit searches all things, even the deep things of God. For who knows a person's thoughts except their own spirit within them? In the same way no one knows the thoughts of God except the Spirit of God. What we have received is not the spirit of the world, but the Spirit who is from God, so that we may understand what God has freely given us. This is what we speak, not in words taught us by human wisdom but in words taught by the Spirit, explaining spiritual realities with Spirit-taught words. The person without the Spirit does not accept the things that come from the Spirit of God but considers them foolishness, and cannot understand them because they are discerned only through the Spirit. The person with the Spirit makes judgments about all things, but such a person

is not subject to merely human judgments, for, "Who has known the mind of the Lord so as to instruct him?" But we have the mind of Christ. (1 Cor. 2:9–16)

The Holy Spirit teaches us limits to our actions and to sin. He teaches us responsibility for ourselves and others. He leads us to grow in grace. He keeps us humble. The Holy Spirit reproves, corrects, teaches, and trains us in righteous living. He provides both guidance and strength. He gives us love, peace, hope, and comfort to endure. The Holy Spirit empowers humankind and gives us self-discipline in dealing with all the things of this world and the spiritual realm (see 2 Tim. 1:7 and Rom. 15:13).

Whether you turn to the right or to the left, your ears will hear a voice behind you, saying, "This is the way; walk in it." (Isa. 30:21; see also John 14:25–26; Matt. 10:19–20; and Luke 12:11–12)

The Holy Spirit gives us wisdom, understanding, knowledge, and all kinds of skills (see Exod. 31:3). Yes, the Holy Spirit teaches, but we have to be willing to learn and to earnestly seek out the help of the Holy Spirit. We cannot understand or comprehend God without a true desire to learn. And once we begin, the floodgates open, and we cannot halt or be full. We want more, and we want to share. The Holy Spirit gives us insight and a craving to know the mysteries of God. Just simply ask, and it will be done (see James 1:5).

*O*BEDIENCE

The Holy Spirit resides within all Christian believers and teaches us obedience to the Word of God. Our bodies are a temple for the Holy Spirit. It is not just important but required for us to respect not only our own body but also those of others. God created you unique to the world, and as such, you need to take the responsibility of caring for yourself and others. In this, God expects absolute obedience (see 1 Cor. 6:19–20).

We are all weak at times and need to take extra care to be obedient to God. Support from other Christians can be helpful and not difficult to find. But also know that prayer is always available to you. It is a way for all of us to be closer to God. Not sure of how to pray? The Holy Spirit is there, already hearing your voiceless pleas. He knows your needs and worries. Know and take comfort in that the Holy Spirit will intercede on your behalf and guide you to obedience (see Rom. 8:26–27).

It is respectful obedience that leads to knowledge and understanding—the beginning of wisdom. When we stop blindly rejecting and fighting the unknown, our minds become clear. The veil of ignorance is removed. What we are open to learning can move us forward into a better future (see Prov. 9:10).

Disobedience causes the Holy Spirit sorrow and distress, like that of a parent and child. It especially hurts God when we are hostile toward one another. A dire warning here: do not test the Holy Spirit, for you will lose. The penalty is great (see Eph. 4:30 and Acts 5:1–10).

There is one sin from which we can never recover. Jesus is very clear in this very serious and important warning to everyone.

> I tell you, every kind of sin and slander can be forgiven, but blasphemy against the Spirit will not be forgiven. Anyone who speaks a word against the Son of Man will be forgiven, but anyone who speaks against the Holy Spirit will not be forgiven, either in this age or in the age to come. (Matt. 12:31–32; see also Heb. 10:29)

TRANSFORMATION

The Holy Spirit is the essence or presence of God in us and in our lives. We are transformed by the power of the Holy Spirit. Through the Holy

Spirit, the Lord's thoughts and actions become ours. And we will know God and come to know His will. Jesus assures us of the power we are to receive through having the Holy Spirit in our lives (see Acts 1:8).

This divine empowerment enables us to become the person God meant for us to be. It evolves and fills every facet of our lives. We begin to accomplish God's purpose for us and to make an impactful difference in the world.

Empowered by the Holy Spirit, you will find yourself seeking Christian fellowship and education. You will develop a desire to share with people about your transformation. Amazing opportunities will present themselves, and you will share—yes, witness to—the miraculous transformation of your life.

This transforming power of the Holy Spirit was demonstrated when Jesus's disciples prayed and then were filled with the Holy Spirit and began their ministries (see Acts 4:31 and 1 Cor. 12:3).

Acceptance of the truth of God's Word results in marvelous inward changes in ourselves. It is with the power of the Holy Spirit that God changes our hearts, attitudes, and actions—the characteristics of ourselves. There are nine inherent characteristics evidenced through one's transformation by the Holy Spirit. They are living characteristics helping us to endure hardships and challenges coming our way.

> The fruit of the Spirit is love, joy, peace, forbearance, kindness, goodness, faithfulness, gentleness and self-control. Against such things there is no law.

> Since we live by the Spirit, let us keep in step with the Spirit. (Gal 5:22–23, 25)

The Holy Spirit bestows fruitful gifts upon each one of us. Each one is different and unique and chosen specifically for each of us. It can be exciting to see exactly how we can use our specialized gifts. We are to fulfill

God's purpose and plan. We are to employ our personalized gifts to the benefit of one another. Simply serve God and serve one another.

> There are different kinds of gifts, but the same Spirit distributes them. There are different kinds of service, but the same Lord. There are different kinds of working, but in all of them and in everyone it is the same God at work.
>
> Now to each one the manifestation of the Spirit is given for the common good. To one there is given through the Spirit a message of wisdom, to another a message of knowledge by means of the same Spirit, to another faith by the same Spirit, to another gifts of healing by that one Spirit, to another miraculous powers, to another prophecy, to another distinguishing between spirits, to another speaking in different kinds of tongues and to still another the interpretation of tongues. All these are the work of one and the same Spirit, and he distributes them to each one, just as he determines. (1 Cor. 12:4–11)

Our hearts are born again through the Holy Spirit. Faith is the result of being born again. It is the divine work of the Holy Spirit (see John 3:3–12). We become renewed, invigorated, and fruitful with the Holy Spirit in our lives.

True transformation is instantaneous and results in positive growth and change. In some individuals, this is a more visible and drastic change in attitude and behavior. Other individuals may have a less dramatic change. But change is inevitable when we are filled with the Holy Spirit. We are filled with a new spiritual life. We experience an enlightenment and the goodness of the Word of God. It is our responsibility to remain steadfast in this new life (see Heb. 6:4–6).

We no longer live under Old Testament law of condemnation and death but rather the transformational new law of the Spirit, of love and life. Accepting this brings you into the family of God, with all its freedoms and promises.

A transformed apostle Paul, who once persecuted Christians, shares the reality of the death sentence brought on by the law of sin and the freedom of life eternal under the law of the Spirit.

> There is now no condemnation for those who are in Christ Jesus, because through Christ Jesus the law of the Spirit who gives life has set you free from the law of sin and death. For what the law was powerless to do because it was weakened by the flesh, God did by sending his own Son in the likeness of sinful flesh to be a sin offering. And so he condemned sin in the flesh, in order that the righteous requirement of the law might be fully met in us, who do not live according to the flesh but according to the Spirit.
>
> Those who live according to the flesh have their minds set on what the flesh desires; but those who live in accordance with the Spirit have their minds set on what the Spirit desires. The mind governed by the flesh is death, but the mind governed by the Spirit is life and peace. The mind governed by the flesh is hostile to God; it does not submit to God's law, nor can it do so. Those who are in the realm of the flesh cannot please God.
>
> You, however, are not in the realm of the flesh but are in the realm of the Spirit, if indeed the Spirit of God lives in you. And if anyone does not have the Spirit of Christ, they do not belong to Christ. But if Christ is in you, then even though your body is subject to death because of sin, the Spirit gives life because of righteousness. And if the Spirit of him who raised Jesus from the dead is living in you, he who raised Christ from the dead will also give life to your mortal bodies because of his Spirit who lives in you.

Therefore, brothers and sisters, we have an obligation—but it is not to the flesh, to live according to it. For if you live according to the flesh, you will die; but if by the Spirit you put to death the misdeeds of the body, you will live.

For those who are led by the Spirit of God are the children of God. The Spirit you received does not make you slaves, so that you live in fear again; rather, the Spirit you received brought about your adoption to sonship. And by him we cry, "Abba, Father." The Spirit himself testifies with our spirit that we are God's children. Now if we are children, then we are heirs—heirs of God and co-heirs with Christ, if indeed we share in his sufferings in order that we may also share in his glory. (Rom. 8:1–17)

Scripture and Disciples

THE BIBLE IS an official document. As the word *document* is defined, it is an official written record of proof—proof in the form of historical recordings of events that occurred and people and places that have existed and still do for the most part. It is an anthology, a compilation of ancient histories of the ancient world generally around the Mediterranean region.

This official document is also the most amazing piece of writing that has ever existed. It is composed of every genre, of every artistic endeavor. There is poetry and song, prayer and pleading, mystery and intrigue, and drama and comedy. Family histories and subsequent trees are outlined throughout the Bible. We can find spies, murderers, romantics, and action heroes. We can follow a protagonist through the winding maze of events, feeling every emotion they have in every encounter.

Once you can begin to understand the parts, the whole becomes more and more clear. The aha moment follows soon after. This is an exciting moment—a profound moment of clarity and insight. It's the feeling that you are being let into a highly secretive world full of incredible benefits—success, happiness, close and renewed relationships, and, best of all, unconditional love.

What is the ultimate purpose of the Bible? The Bible is an account of God's quest for a relationship with humankind. It begins in Genesis, where God creates the sum total of existence and his mysterious plan is set in motion (see 1 Cor. 2:7 and Col. 1:26–27). The histories relayed throughout scripture reveal humankind's reactions to God and God's responses in reaching out to fallen humans. It is through the narrative of God's relationship with humanity that humankind's history is laid out—from creation to the eternal existence of a new world with God or eternal death without God.

God reveals a lot about himself through scripture. The mystery of God is revealed through Jesus Christ, who is the living Word of God. The mystery has been kept secret since the world began and made manifest in and through scripture. God reveals all to us as we continue in our faithful obedience to studying and following his Word.

> All of our praise rises to the One who is strong enough to make you strong, exactly as preached in Jesus Christ, precisely as revealed in the mystery kept secret for so long but now an open book through the prophetic Scriptures. All the nations of the world can now know the truth and be brought into obedient belief, carrying out the orders of God, who got all this started, down to the very last letter. (Rom. 16:25–26 MSG)

The Bible is truth written with the divine inspiration of God. It was written by individuals under the direct influence of the Holy Spirit. It is not secular but rather a revelation of God's heart and mind and must be approached with this understanding. It has and will continue to endure forever (see Ps. 33:4–6).

The Bible has been studied by the greatest minds for many hundreds of years. It is more than just a book. It is both enlightening and inspirational. Its precepts and moral principles are truly life-giving and life-saving. It has layers and layers of insights. History's most exceptional thinkers changed the world through the profound insights existing within its pages.

In fact, the Bible inspired the birth of the American nation. It is what the United States Constitution is based upon—"one Nation under God, indivisible, with liberty and justice for all."

The Bible outlines proper behavior for ourselves and our relationships with and responsibilities for others, including God. We have placed our hopes and dreams in the security of God's Word (see Ps. 119:114 MSG).

The Bible is divided into books, chapters, and numerically labeled verses. It is meant to be studied and shared among people everywhere. Hence it is designed to facilitate this. If you wish to discuss a particular story, idea, or concept with someone, you can tell them exactly where to look, right down to a specific verse. This works regardless of the translation.

Different translations speak differently to everyone but relay the exact same facts and concepts. I personally like to use at least four different translations to clarify particular passages I am studying. There are many translations available, and only you can decide with which one(s) you are comfortable. But it can be good to use several different translations of scripture. This will help establish a clarity of meaning for you.

A dictionary is also very helpful to define biblical terms, even commonly used words. You might be surprised as to how influential and vital the definitions of specific words can become. The entire meaning of a passage emerges in greater clarity with the right descriptor or explanation. I use both a regular dictionary and a biblical dictionary. I am just beginning to use books on systematic theology, which go into much greater detail on topics and doctrines within the Bible.

One of my favorite study books has always been a Bible reader's companion given to me by my mother when I was a teenager. It includes details of historical and geographical significance for each book and chapter within the Bible. It helps to make sense of what was happening in the area at the time of the specific event and at the time of the writing.

The Bible is filled with so much information, and each time one revisits a chapter, more and more is revealed. Each topic is complex but simply explained. The clear and concise wording leads the reader into deeper meaning and life application. It is written in straightforward language and truths. Yet within each sentence or paragraph, there is always a deeper core of ideology and meaning. Ultimately, it is the Holy Spirit who will begin to remove the veil of ignorance from our eyes. So, let's keep reading and studying and praying for enlightenment (see Josh. 1:8 NLT).

A lot of the New Testament writings are a repetition of key concepts in Christianity. Most come in the form of letters and Gospels (the good news). They were presented to many different individuals and groups across the land as the apostles spread the message of Jesus. The four Gospel accounts, Matthew, Mark, Luke, and John, repeat many of the same stories because these apostles were present together for the same events and received the same messages from Jesus. And really, some of us need this repetition before we experience the aha moment of clarity and insight.

We all learn and assimilate information in different ways. Some are visual or auditory or do best when writing down information. A good study guide based on any one book of the Bible or covering specific topics is a great way to begin your studies of scripture. Joining a Bible study group is very helpful as you learn and discuss scripture together.

The apostles, the original twelve disciples of Jesus, had so much to share with us and so little time. Because of this, the apostle John stated that he knew he had to be very selective about what he included in his writings. He chose to bring something important and meaningful for each one of us. He was filled with and inspired by the Holy Spirit to complete this task (see John 21:25 and John 20:30)

TEACHING AND CORRECTING

Scripture makes it easier to follow the path God has chosen for each of us. How we are to behave ourselves and how we are to behave toward others are both outlined in direct statements. They can also be discerned within stories and parables. In learning appropriate behaviors, we equip ourselves to be more successful in our lives and in the lives of others. Becoming productive members of society is a goal with many benefits.

> All Scripture is God-breathed and is useful for teaching, rebuking, correcting and training in righteousness, so that the servant of God may be thoroughly equipped for every good work. (2 Tim. 3:16–17; see also Isa. 48:17)

Being a parent comes with certain obligations. We must be the primary teachers of our children. We are expected to teach them how to behave and to correct them when they do not do this well. Scripture outlines the importance of raising our children in the instruction and correction of the Lord (see Eph. 6:4). Nobody wants to be around a child who misbehaves and requires continual correction or discipline. Those children usually grow up to be the same type of person in adulthood. We all must begin this teaching early. The Bible has clear guidelines for raising pleasant and righteous children (see Heb. 12:4–11 MSG and Prov. 15:10).

Scripture clearly outlines the discipline of the Lord. We must be knowingly responsible and accountable for all we think, say, and do. This applies to us as well as our children. We have a moral obligation to conform to what is right and good. The results are great for us and society as a whole. It is the difference between success and happiness and death and sorrow.

Scripture is not just a retelling of history or simply an outline of how we should behave. It strives to encourage us. It guides us. It brings to us an assurance of hope and a purpose, which inspires faith, obedience, and endurance. It keeps future generations from "groping in the darkness" (see Job 12:25). Scripture is not just a history of the past but a revelation of actions to be evaluated to make a better future (see Rom. 15:4 NLT).

Scripture provides a valuable map for lost people. We cannot make it out of this terrifying wilderness on our own. Never be afraid to ask for help or directions. We all must stop being self-centered and stubborn. We cannot do everything by ourselves. Our knowledge is very limited. The Bible is an instruction manual and a road map for humankind while we remain on this earth. Just as with the road map of the town where you live, there is no room for deviation from scripture. It is specific in its instruction. Written in the past, it prepares us for surviving the present and the future.

> Go now and write all this down. Put it in a book so that the record will be there to instruct the coming generations, because this is a rebel generation, a people who lie, a people unwilling to listen to anything God tells them. They tell their spiritual leaders, "Don't bother us with irrelevancies." They tell their preachers, "Don't waste our time on impracticalities. Tell us what makes us feel better. Don't bore us with obsolete religion. That stuff means nothing to us. Quit hounding us." (Isa. 30:8–11 MSG)

The Holy Scriptures, both the Old and New Testaments, bring us wisdom and warnings (see 2 Tim. 3:15; 1 Cor. 10:11 NLT; and Prov. 5:1–2). They bring us knowledge and teach us discretion. We must learn from the past in order to make a better future. Our spiritual maturity develops through our successes and mistakes and those of people from long ago. It is important that we continually return to study scripture to refresh and educate. You will make new discoveries with each reading, even if it's the same verses read previously, numerous times.

I cannot end this section without mentioning the eloquent and powerful book of Psalms. The book of Psalms was written by King David to teach the generations to come about all the goodness of the Lord—his perfect character and his wonderful, loving works for all humankind. They are beautifully written and well worth a reflective read.

> My people, hear my teaching; listen to the words of my mouth. I will open my mouth with a parable; I will utter hidden things, things from of old—things we have heard and known, things our ancestors have told us. We will not hide them from their descendants; we will tell the next generation the praiseworthy deeds of the Lord, his power, and the wonders he has done. He decreed statutes for Jacob and established the law in Israel, which he commanded our ancestors to teach their children, so the next generation would know them, even the children yet to be born, and they in turn would tell their children. Then they would put their trust in God and would not forget his deeds but would keep his commands. (Ps. 78:1–7)

APPLICATION

The Bible is very visible, tangible, and personal. God teaches us through his words. God nourishes our hearts and strengthens our spirits to be able to apply his truths to our daily lives. Scripture reveals the hope from the past and the faith for the future. It is replete with testimonials of living day by day through personal accounts of real events. We learn to live by example. It directs us to discover our own hope and seize our own faith for the future. We need to understand that practicing what we learn from scripture will take time (see Jer. 15:16 NLT).

Through study and prayer, we can gain entrance into scripture and begin a relationship with God. It is in scripture that we can know the will of God and the purpose he has for each one of us. We have been given the Holy Spirit, who lives within every Christian, to bring clarity, understanding, and application of God's Word to our lives. Ask the Holy Spirit to come into your life, and he will guide you through scripture and the application of it to your life (see Ps. 119:129–136; Ps. 119:124–128 MSG; and Matt 4:4 MSG).

God feeds our soul through his Word. We must be patient though, for God speaks to us through scripture using the Holy Spirit as he sees fit for each one of us. We grow and mature at God's pace. It's God's plan and his timetable.

Scripture facilitates our spiritual and emotional growth. We need to study and to constantly grow in our understanding of God and his purpose for our lives. And by practicing what we learn, we can incorporate it naturally into our daily lives (see James 1:22–25 and Ps. 119:89–96 MSG).

There is a freedom available to us in living the Word of God. This does not mean we are free to live doing whatever we want. That way of living can often destroy our God-given freedom (see Rom 6:17 MSG). We must approach it with faithful obedience and a commitment to incorporate it honestly into our lives. Integrity in living God's truth will save lives, including yours.

Scripture outlines the conditions of our relationships with others. We are to act with humility, peace, and for the good of all. We are to encourage and motivate others. We reveal our true character by how we edify others. Scripture helps direct us in how to do so with the same mind-set as Jesus (see Phil. 2:2–5; Prov. 3:27; Rom. 12:181; and Thess. 4:18 NLT).

Solomon, son of King David, wrote the book of Proverbs to teach us how to live among one another on earth. It is truly a book of wisdom to learn by.

> [The purpose of Scripture is] for gaining wisdom and instruction; for understanding words of insight; for receiving instruction in prudent behavior, doing what is right and just and fair; for giving prudence to those who are simple, knowledge and discretion to the young— let the wise listen and add to their learning, and let the discerning get guidance—for understanding proverbs and parables, the sayings and riddles of the wise. The fear of

the Lord is the beginning of knowledge, but fools despise wisdom and instruction. (Prov. 1:2–7; see also the MSG translation)

ARABLES

Jesus used parables to teach heavenly truths to a human audience. We tend to see things in concrete, observable terms and, hence, miss the abstract heavenly messages (see John 3:12). His stories encourage us and teach us how to grow and mature spiritually, emotionally, and intellectually. They teach character development in relation to God and other people based on love and not law.

All that Jesus teaches comes directly from God (see John 15:15). Not everyone is ready to hear or understand the messages contained in these stories. We must pray that the Holy Spirit will lift the veil of ignorance, which hardens hearts and blinds minds to God's Word.

The three apostles, Matthew, Mark, and Luke, all tell similar stories of Jesus explaining why he often spoke in parables when teaching the crowds of people who came to hear him. All three explain a lack of one's readiness similarly. Our hearts must be prepared to not only hear but also accept the truth coming from the Word of God.

> The disciples came up and asked, "Why do you tell stories?'"
>
> [Jesus] replied, "You've been given insight into God's kingdom. You know how it works. Not everybody has this gift, this insight; it hasn't been given to them. Whenever someone has a ready heart for this, the insights and understandings flow freely. But if there is no readiness, any trace of receptivity soon disappears. That's why I tell stories: to create readiness, to nudge the people toward receptive insight. In their present state they can stare till

doomsday and not see it, listen till they're blue in the face and not get it. I don't want Isaiah's forecast repeated all over again: 'Your ears are open but you don't hear a thing. Your eyes are awake but you don't see a thing. The people are blockheads! They stick their fingers in their ears so they won't have to listen; They screw their eyes shut so they won't have to look, so they won't have to deal with me face-to-face and let me heal them."

But you have God-blessed eyes—eyes that see! And God-blessed ears—ears that hear! A lot of people, prophets and humble believers among them, would have given anything to see what you are seeing, to hear what you are hearing, but never had the chance. (Matt. 13:10–17 MSG; see also Isa. 42:20 NLT; Mark 4:10–20, 33–34 MSG; Luke 8:10–15 MSG; and Isa. 6:8–13 NLT)

$\mathcal{P}$ROPHECY AND FALSE PROPHETS

Prophecy is meant to encourage and challenge us. But we must be Christ focused and not sign focused. Check your perspectives, priorities, and pursuits. You should know demonic and deceiving sources are often present in psychic events and occult practices (see Acts 16:16–19).

God's truths are not found in strange new doctrines or new age philosophies. These are contrary to basic New Testament teachings. You can often identify a fake through their actions, which always defines their character. Scripture is very clear as to what happens if we turn to mediums and spiritualists instead of God. We become disobedient and unclean. Unclean literally means to "pollute your soul." Both the false individuals and the unclean followers will face the severe punishment of God in the end (see 1 John 4:1; Heb. 13:8–9; 1 Chron. 10:13–14 MSG; Lev. 19:31; Deut. 18:10–12; and Lev. 20:6).

Maintain your focus in the Word of God. Place it deep within your heart and soul. His Word is reliable and a guide through this ever-darkening world. Jesus Christ is the light through it all. True prophecy is God inspired and revealed through the Holy Spirit. Always know you can call upon the Holy Spirit to help you discern the truth around you (see 2 Pet. 1:19–21).

> Be wary of false preachers who smile a lot, dripping with practiced sincerity. Chances are they are out to rip you off some way or other. Don't be impressed with charisma; look for character. Who preachers are is the main thing, not what they say. A genuine leader will never exploit your emotions or your pocketbook. (Matt. 7:15–19 MSG)

OBEDIENCE

Obey the Word of God, for the true character of your heart is known. Remember, God is omniscient. He knows everything. He knows our thoughts and our actions, even before we think or act. He knows us thoroughly and intimately. We will be judged according to what we exhibit to the world (see Heb. 4:12).

Pay attention to and trust in the Word of God. It's important you *be still* and listen for God's direction. We tend to miss these a lot! You cannot obey what you cannot see or hear.

> Trust God from the bottom of your heart; don't try to figure out everything on your own. Listen for God's voice in everything you do, everywhere you go; he's the one who will keep you on track. Don't assume you know it all. Run to God! (Prov. 3:5–7 MSG)

Be truthful and accountable. Integrity is important. Your character is on view for God and everyone. Maintain your honor and respect in the eyes of God, and you will receive this from other people. It is important to not trip up others on their path through this difficult world. Show them the reason for the hope you have in God's Word through your actions (see 2 Cor. 4:2–4 and 1 Pet. 1:22–25 MSG).

$\mathcal{A}$POSTLES AND DISCIPLES

What is the difference between an apostle and a disciple? Apostles were eyewitnesses of Jesus Christ. They were God-chosen individuals, given a divine commission and divine authority, and sent out on a mission to spread the gospel message of Jesus.

The word *disciple* comes from the Latin meaning "learner." Disciples are divinely chosen individuals who follow the teachings of Jesus Christ with faith and obedience—in other words, true Christians like us. Some are teachers, and all are students of the gospel.

We are forever the students of the Bible. We are expected to be active participants in our learning and in our teaching of others. We are sent out into the world to share our faith and demonstrate examples of righteous living. But, first and always, we require continuous study of God's Word and an attitude of belief and obedience as disciples of Jesus. This means maintaining a focus on being Christlike in all we think, say, and do (see Mark 8:34 and Luke 9:23–24).

There were twelve original disciples of Jesus. Several were apostolic witnesses to the resurrection of Jesus Christ. Additionally, several of the original twelve were divinely inspired to write the New Testament of the Bible.

All are and have been ordinary people who do and did extraordinary things in the name of Jesus. They are or have been God's opportunity for spreading his ministry of redemption and reconciliation—of love. Apostles like Paul built the foundations for the church and Christian living. Paul explains to us in great clarity his part and ours in God's plan:

This is why I, Paul, am in jail for Christ, having taken up the cause of you outsiders, so-called. I take it that you're familiar with the part I was given in God's plan for including everybody. I got the inside story on this from God himself, as I just wrote you in brief.

As you read over what I have written to you, you'll be able to see for yourselves into the mystery of Christ. None of our ancestors understood this. Only in our time has it been made clear by God's Spirit through his holy apostles and prophets of this new order. The mystery is that people who have never heard of God and those who have heard of him all their lives (what I've been calling outsiders and insiders) stand on the same ground before God. They get the same offer, same help, same promises in Christ Jesus. The Message is accessible and welcoming to everyone, across the board.

This is my life work: helping people understand and respond to this Message. It came as a sheer gift to me, a real surprise, God handling all the details. When it came to presenting the Message to people who had no background in God's way, I was the least qualified of any of the available Christians. God saw to it that I was equipped, but you can be sure that it had nothing to do with my natural abilities.

And so here I am, preaching and writing about things that are way over my head, the inexhaustible riches and generosity of Christ. My task is to bring out in the open and make plain what God, who created all this in the first place, has been doing in secret and behind the scenes all along. Through followers of Jesus like yourselves gathered in churches, this extraordinary plan of God is becoming known and talked about even among the angels!

> All this is proceeding along lines planned all along by God and then executed in Christ Jesus. When we trust in him, we're free to say whatever needs to be said, bold to go wherever we need to go. So don't let my present trouble on your behalf get you down. Be proud! (Eph. 3:1–13 MSG; see also Eph. 1:9 NLT)

THE COMMISSION

The first apostles were sent out into the world to spread the good news of redemption and reconciliation through Jesus Christ. This event is called the Great Commission because it was the resurrected Jesus himself who instructed his disciples to actively make disciples of all nations (see Matt. 28:16–20 and John 20:19–22). These individuals had firsthand experience of the Lord Jesus Christ and his teachings. They became martyrs because of their knowledge of the truth and their willingness to share that truth. We need to realize that *absolutely nobody* would willingly experience such intense torture and suffering as they did for anything less than the truth. Definitely not for a lie (see Luke 11:49).

The first disciples were obedient to Jesus and his charge to take care of God's people. They knew their vital task was twofold. They were to teach about God's plan of forgiveness for trespasses and his free gift of eternal life. And they were to offer every person an intimate relationship with God. They understood that everyone must be given a choice, a chance. And those brave people devoted their lives to see that every one of us has an opportunity to hear the good news (see Matt. 10:1–8).

Many of the disciples did indeed perform miracles in the name of Jesus. We can witness miracles even today. God works in us and through us today just as he did yesterday (see Acts 3:1–10, 16; 6:8; 8:6–7; 9:17–18; 9:33–41; 14:8–10; 15:12; 16:16–19; 19:11–12; 20:9–12; and 28:7–9).

> After the Lord Jesus had spoken to them, he was taken
> up into heaven and he sat at the right hand of God. Then
> the disciples went out and preached everywhere, and the
> Lord worked with them and confirmed his word by the
> signs that accompanied it. (Mark 16:19–20)

We are all commanded to become disciples of Christ, to learn and to teach his Word. God made this possible, and the original twelve apostles paved the way. It is still, to this day, not an easy task. Some people are persecuted and slain for their attempts to teach the good news. But at least they have remained obedient to God even to death, as was Jesus (see Luke 10:3).

Being a Christian can be difficult in this world. The first disciples experienced this firsthand in their own times. The reality is that Jesus does not abandon us to our own devices. He has given us the Holy Spirit to teach, guide, and protect us. Through the Holy Spirit, Jesus equips us to be his disciples. Therefore, put your faith and trust in God. He is faithful in fulfilling all his promises to us (see Matt. 5:10–12).

> [Jesus said], "I am the vine; you are the branches. If you
> remain in me and I in you, you will bear much fruit; apart
> from me you can do nothing.
>
> "If you remain in me and my words remain in you, ask
> whatever you wish, and it will be done for you. This is
> to my Father's glory, that you bear much fruit, showing
> yourselves to be my disciples." (John 15:5, 7–8)

We are always dependent on God. It is through him and the inner workings of his plan that we can accomplish so much. We are responsible for showing the world the reason for our hope in a blessed future. The world will recognize and come to know Jesus by our actions. We must set good examples of righteous behavior for others to want to follow. Our words and deeds demonstrate our focus as disciples of Christ. There is one main assignment Jesus requires of us as his disciples—to love (see John 13:34–35).

FREEDOM FOR RECONCILIATION

There is indeed a freedom in following what Jesus taught and teaches all his disciples. We are no longer slaves to an uncertain life and a certain death. We begin to learn and understand the truth of reality—of existence. This knowledge of the truth comes with great freedom and great rewards (see John 8:31–32).

Believe and act with faithful obedience to God. The severed relationship will then be restored. There will be an eternal place for you with God in heaven. Jesus gives us, as his disciples, hope and comfort in this knowledge when he says:

> "Do not let your hearts be troubled. You believe in God; believe also in me. My Father's house has many rooms; if that were not so, would I have told you that I am going there to prepare a place for you? And if I go and prepare a place for you, I will come back and take you to be with me that you also may be where I am." (John 14:1–3)

Look around. Observe what is happening. The world is rushing toward Judgment Day. Read scripture and become prepared. To be ready, believers must serve God actively, and nonbelievers must make peace with God before it's too late. God is committed to a reconciliation, a renewed relationship with each of us. The invitation is there (see 2 Cor. 5:19–20).

Covenants and Commandments

A COVENANT IS not a contract but rather a promise with God. A covenant with God comes with certain privileges and obligations. And through these, we have a renewed bond with God. It is the commandments that come with a covenant, which outline the responsibilities we must maintain in our part of a sacred oath. But they are not simply rules conferred to us. Rather, they are specific points that delineate a guidance system for navigating through a successful life on earth in order to achieve the goal of a spectacular life in heaven.

A covenant establishes a particular relationship between two parties. Synonymous with covenant is an alliance or union. The word *covenant* comes from the Latin meaning "a coming together." God establishes covenants to encourage a personal relationship with him. It is a reunion with him out of a promise of love and not out of a fear of punishment. God can be the best father any of us will ever have (see Ps. 25:14 NLT). His covenant seals this loving relationship.

Remember that *fear* often should be understood as reverence and respect in terms of our relationship with God. He makes a promise to us that is fulfilled if we remain trusting and obedient to him. For us, it is a commitment sealed in Christ's blood and entered into through our working toward achieving righteousness. It is righteous individuals who have a moral and just character, free from guilt or sin. This is a worthy goal for a pleasant and satisfying life and salvation for the eternal life to come.

God created a binding covenant of salvation for us and for our children through his Son, Jesus Christ. We can trust in this. We know and take comfort in the fact that God must continually intervene to ensure both his promises and purposes are fulfilled. He is our savior with a plan.

> When people take an oath, they call on someone greater than themselves to hold them to it. And without any question that oath is binding. God also bound himself with an oath, so that those who received the promise could be perfectly sure that he would never change his mind. So God has given both his promise and his oath. These two things are unchangeable because it is impossible for God to lie. Therefore, we who have fled to him for refuge can have great confidence as we hold to the hope that lies before us. This hope is a strong and trustworthy anchor for our souls. It leads us through the curtain into God's inner sanctuary. (Heb. 6:16–19 NLT)

COVENANTS IN THE BEGINNING

The shedding of blood was an integral part of covenants with God in the Old Testament. In Genesis 4:21, the first covenant was made with humans—the shedding of blood for Adam. In Genesis chapters 6 through 9, the story of Noah illustrates the return of order to humanity through the shedding of the blood of humankind and then the establishment of a covenant between God and every living creature. The rainbow is set in the heavens by God as a symbol of this promise for the floodwaters to never again destroy all life on the earth.

We also find God had made everlasting individual covenants with each of the patriarchs of Judaism—Abraham, Isaac, and Jacob. These men demonstrated consistent faith, trust, and obedience to God. In return, God promised that they would have land and offspring abundant. It is through these covenants that God also promised them forgiveness, protection, and an intimate, personal relationship with all their descendants thereafter (see Gen. 12:3; 17:7; and 17:13).

There is an importance in learning about God's covenant with Abraham. This particular covenant coincides with his promise to us later found in New Testament scripture. It was by Abraham's faith that the most important covenant was made with God. Through Abraham's line, there would come the salvation of the world—Jesus Christ.

There needs to be an understanding about faith. Faith can never be required by any agreement, rule, or law, or it would not be faith. There cannot be any outside regulation whatsoever of honest, emotional gifts. Faith must be freely given and freely demonstrated. Harmony must exist between the faith of humankind being given freely to God and the free gift of grace by God to those who are faithful to him (see Rom. 4:13–16).

Faith and obedience to God is evidence of our trust in his covenant with us and our desire for a personal relationship with him. We should strive to become righteous individuals in the eyes of God. This is a meaningful way to actively demonstrate our faith in our praises for all God does for us.

It was King David who wrote a heartfelt song to God, revealing his own understanding of the fullness or benefits of God's commands. Unfortunately, David was intellectually and emotionally operating under the old law of conditional, regulation-empowered actions. Now we are under the new law of unconditional, grace-enabled behaviors brought to us through the resurrection of Jesus. Fortunately, the law has changed for our benefit since David's time. The covenants of God have not changed, but the law has.

> O Lord, listen to my cry; give me the discerning mind you
> promised. Listen to my prayer; rescue me as you promised.
> Let praise flow from my lips, for you have taught me
> your decrees. Let my tongue sing about your word, for all

your commands are right. Give me a helping hand, for I have chosen to follow your commandments. O Lord, I have longed for your rescue, and your instructions are my delight. Let me live so I can praise you, and may your regulations help me. I have wandered away like a lost sheep; come and find me, for I have not forgotten your commands. (Ps. 119:169–176 NLT)

THE OLD LAW

The Ten Commandments became the law given to Moses by God. Of the Ten Commandments, the first four are about loving God, and the last six are about loving others. The high priests of the Old Testament created an additional 613 laws to rule over the people. These 613 commands or laws written in the Torah are considered to fall within subcategories of the Ten Commandments. Of these, 248 are affirmative (do this), and 365 are negative (don't do that).

It is through all these laws that humankind became trapped in the cycle of sin. Old Testament laws defined sin—made us know sin. We could not escape this human-created prison to become righteous individuals in the eyes of God (see Rom. 3:20).

Old Testament law binds our gift of free will. It enslaves us, taking away our freedoms. We become fearful of doing anything for anyone. This often leads to apathy. Anxiety and depression can follow the stressors of living under such repressive, oppressive constraints. For one thing, it states that if you break one law, you have broken them all (see James 2:10).

Furthermore, humankind became the judge, jury, and executioner under the old laws. And all it took was two or more witnesses to convict a person of breaking a law (see Heb. 10:28). Sound familiar for us today?

Paul explains Old Testament law quite eloquently. Old Testament law brings wrath, guilt, insecurity, and alienation. It also effectuates punishment and death.

What shall we say, then? Is the law sinful? Certainly not! Nevertheless, I would not have known what sin was had it not been for the law. For I would not have known what coveting really was if the law had not said, "You shall not covet." But sin, seizing the opportunity afforded by the commandment, produced in me every kind of coveting. For apart from the law, sin was dead. Once I was alive apart from the law; but when the commandment came, sin sprang to life and I died. I found that the very commandment that was intended to bring life actually brought death. For sin, seizing the opportunity afforded by the commandment, deceived me, and through the commandment put me to death. (Rom. 7:7–11)

THE NEW COVENANT

It is in the Old Testament that we learn of God's covenant with King David (see 2 Sam. 7:16). This laid the foundation for the expectation of Jesus the Messiah and a new rule that was to come (see Gal. 4:4–5). The old law was to be replaced by a new, better law.

"The day is coming," says the Lord, "when I will make a new covenant with the people of Israel and Judah. This covenant will not be like the one I made with their ancestors when I took them by the hand and brought them out of the land of Egypt. They broke that covenant, though I loved them as a husband loves his wife," says the Lord.

"But this is the new covenant I will make with the people of Israel after those days," says the Lord. "I will put my instructions deep within them, and I will write them on their hearts. I will be their God, and they will be my people. And they will not need to teach their neighbors, nor will they need to teach their relatives, saying, 'You should know the Lord.' For everyone, from the least to the greatest, will know me already," says the Lord. "And I will forgive their wickedness, and I will never again remember their sins." (Jeremiah 31:31–34 NLT)

The New Testament of the Bible outlines the new covenant in detail. Through this new covenant, God sets about to recover and to redeem his children. We have been offered the opportunity for life through our justification by faith and freedom through our righteous actions. This removes the old rule of death through punishment and slavery to sin. We now can operate under the new law of grace and truth (see John 1:17 and Acts 13:38–39).

Through the death and resurrection of Christ, God canceled the written code with its regulations. They were nailed to the cross. The blood of Christ abolished the law of commandments and ordinances and washed away our crimes. The old law is done. Our bindings have been severed. We have found freedom in the new covenant through Jesus Christ (see Col. 2:13–15 and 1 Cor. 15:51–57).

The new covenant of God was created through the sacrificial blood of the pure, unblemished Lamb of God. This covenant is sealed in the blood of Jesus, as was required in the Old Testament times. This sacrificial offering removed our certainty of punishment and death and has given us the promise of impunity and everlasting life. Jesus Christ laid down his life to bring us freedom in the new covenant. We remember and honor him for doing this when we celebrate Communion or the Lord's Supper (see 1 Cor. 11:25 and Mark 14:24 NLT).

Jesus gave us a new commandment of love that did away with all other laws. The new covenant of love frees us from sin, anger, and hate. We are no longer under the law but under the commitment of grace and righteousness, which are the results of love.

There are no benefits to living sinful lives. Under the old law of sin, sins are punished and death is the reward. The new law is clear: our sins were borne by Jesus Christ, and our debts and punishments were paid for by him. We are no longer slaves to sin but become slaves to righteousness. Our reward for following the new command to love is a pleasant and productive life on earth and an eternity in the glories of heaven (see Rom. 6:15–23 and Ps. 119:93 NLT).

The greatest commandments in the old Mosaic law were replaced by a new royal law of love. There is no longer a lengthy list of dos and don'ts to remember, merely one subject in two parts. Jesus directs us to:

> "Love the Lord your God with all your heart and with all your soul and with all your mind." This is the first and greatest commandment. And the second is like it: "Love your neighbor as yourself." All the Law and the Prophets hang on these two commandments. (Matt. 22:37–40; see also Matt. 7:12; Luke 10:25–27; John 13:34; and Rom. 13:9–10 NLT)

THE NEW RELATIONSHIP

Our relationship with God has become wonderfully changed and personalized through a new, far better covenant than the old one. The importance of his sacrifice was great, but his love for us greater. A close, personal relationship with each one of us was important to his grand plan. While most of us would have preferred a different route, God is omnipotent and knew what was best for getting our attention, respect, and love (see Gal. 2:19–21).

> In fact the ministry Jesus has received is as superior to theirs [the high priests of the old law] as the covenant of which he is mediator is superior to the old one, since the new covenant is established on better promises.

> For if there had been nothing wrong with that first covenant, no place would have been sought for another. But God found fault with the people and said:
>
> "The days are coming," declares the Lord, "when I will make a new covenant with the people of Israel and with the people of Judah. It will not be like the covenant I made with their ancestors when I took them by the hand to lead them out of Egypt, because they did not remain faithful to my covenant, and I turned away from them," declares the Lord. "This is the covenant I will establish with the people of Israel after that time," declares the Lord. "I will put my laws in their minds and write them on their hearts. I will be their God, and they will be my people. No longer will they teach their neighbor, or say to one another, 'Know the Lord,' because they will all know me, from the least of them to the greatest. For I will forgive their wickedness and will remember their sins no more."
>
> By calling this covenant "new," he has made the first one obsolete; and what is obsolete and outdated will soon disappear. (Heb. 8:6–13; see also 2 Cor. 5:17)

We cannot remain trapped in the old way of thinking about God. We can sometimes become so entrenched in our former ways of thought and behavior that it can be a struggle to change. But we must make changes to avoid becoming permanently alienated from God and to begin really living—really living a happy and fruitful life (see Matt. 15:6; Gal. 5:4–6; and Gal. 6:13–15).

As we receive our new relationship with God, we can be confident that we have unconditional love and forgiveness from him. We are guided by the new covenant toward maturity and righteousness. Ultimately, it is God calling us to salvation and our responding in faith that determines our ultimate future direction—life or death.

*F*REEDOM AND LIFE

There is a sense of freedom from judgment and a desire to be fruitful under the new law of love. This is such a stark contrast to living under the paralyzing effects of the old law. God has released us from the old law of sin and death. He has united us in a family of faith that inspires all our actions through love. We are now truly living in the Spirit of the new law (see 2 Cor. 3:6; Rom. 7:4–6 NLT; and Eph. 6:7).

We are no longer to be slaves to the old law but free to be forgiven of our sins and to live a righteous life with the help of the Holy Spirit (see Rom. 8:1–2). When we are filled with the Holy Spirit, we can't help but want to serve and do good things for other people. This need does not come from any requirement, rule, or law. It is the result of the love and gratitude for the Lord growing and maturing within us. We truly have a new freedom in our faith, and our hearts can't help but need to share and to serve (see Mark 10:45 NLT).

No attempts at working hard or at being good enough will lead to our salvation or true happiness. Righteousness is never gained through the law but through faith in Jesus Christ. God has given us what we needed. This is why Jesus came to die for us—to give us a chance at a real life and a renewed and trusting relationship with God. Nothing else is needed to show we are worthy of God's grace and salvation. It came as a free gift through the new covenant. For we are now love motivated versus law regulated in all we think, say, and do (see Gal. 2:16 and Phil. 3:8–9). We can now die to the old law and live with Christ in us. We can live with purpose and a new perspective. We are no longer self-centered but Christ renewed.

OBEDIENCE IN THE NEW COVENANT

God created a single command of love and put an end to the old Mosaic law with its commandments and regulations. He expects obedience and acceptance of everyone under his new commandment of love. Peace among all people is required and achievable under this one command. Why would anyone not want this (see Eph. 2:14–15 NLT)?

The old law was of the world and valueless. We are called to refrain from creating and following strict rules to reign in our fleshly desires (see Col. 2:20–23). This has already been done and failed. No, it is only by completely submitting, handing over control of our lives to God that we are able to follow the new covenant. We are called to be Christlike.

The new command given to us is simple—to act with pure love and reap God's blessings. It is only possible when we submit in faithful obedience to God. In doing this, we glorify him. This is why we were created.

> Blessed is the one who does not walk in step with the wicked or stand in the way that sinners take or sit in the company of mockers, but whose delight is in the law of the Lord, and who meditates on his law day and night. That person is like a tree planted by streams of water, which yields its fruit in season and whose leaf does not whither—whatever they do prospers. (Ps. 1:1–3; see also Ps. 119:33–34; and Prov. 14:22)

In the Old Testament, we waited on God. Now God chooses to wait on us. We do at times try the patience of God (see Isa. 7:13). But he is patient for our sake (see 2 Pet. 3:9 NLT). We should be thankful he waits on us. God's desire is to grant every single one of us salvation (see 2 Pet. 3:15) and to have a personal relationship with all (see Mic. 6:8 and Ps. 103:17–18 NLT). God gives us the freedom to choose.

God offers us a chance to have a meaningful life and a loving relationship with him. It's an individual's freedom of choice to respond in faith to God's new covenant of love. It is a life-or-death decision—a life-or-death choice. What is your choice?

> Now all has been heard; here is the conclusion of the matter: Fear God and keep his commandments, for this is the duty of all mankind. For God will bring every deed into judgment, including every hidden thing, whether it is good or evil. (Eccles. 12:13–14)

Earthly versus Heavenly Focus

HOW WE LIVE is so much more important than where or with what any of us could dream or desire. True happiness and security come from God, not accumulated material things. Jesus asks us to store up our treasures in heaven where they cannot be destroyed or stolen. He questions who we serve. Are we so devoted to serving our carnal lusts out of greed that we forget to serve God and one another out of love? Our hearts will follow where we keep what we treasure. We should be treasuring our families and communities. God knows all else of what we need—food, clothing, shelter. He will always provide for both our physical and spiritual needs (see Matt. 6:19–21, 24–33 NLT; Luke 12:23–31 NLT; and Luke 16:13).

We can't avoid it. The subject of human needs and desires is valuable to discuss along one's Christian journey. It is considered often throughout scripture. It is a part of our human nature to want things and to worry about meeting our personal necessities and carnal cravings. Ultimately, it is where we put our faith and trust that really matters to our lives.

What is it you believe you require, need, or treasure? Understand that most of us are trapped into thinking the material things of this world are essential elements of this life. We can become so anxious about the basic things like needing food and clothing. And we can become slaves to so desperately wanting the stuff we see or hear about in advertisements or at our neighbor's house.

Are you worried about how your friends and neighbors will judge you, based on what you have or haven't got (see Prov. 29:25 MSG)? Do you find real joy or satisfaction from competing with others for who has the latest gadgets? It is really the focus of one's heart and selfless thinking that is of concern here.

Life is more than collecting concrete things. God knows we have needs and yet so much more. He sees to all our needs, including our spiritual ones. We will never truly be lacking for anything (see John 6:35). If we seek to put God at the center of our lives, he will provide for what we really need. Have faith in his promises to see to our true needs and to throw in some desired rewards as well. We forget to trust God and to look to the ultimate value of the eternally existing treasures that can be ours in heaven. Heavenly treasures are the things to which we should give priority in our lives.

Material treasures are fleeting and unreliable. Put God's kingdom first, and you will store up a multitude of treasures lasting an eternity. Let your heart be your guide as to what is worthy of your devotion and adoration. It is your heart that leads the direction of your life (see Luke 12:34; Ezek. 36:26; Prov. 4:23; and Ps. 73:1–28 MSG).

> He who did not spare his own Son, but gave him up for us all—how will he not also, along with him, graciously give us all things? (Rom. 8:32)

GREED

Greed is found in both the wealthy and the poor. It is the frame of mind or status of the heart that gives life real meaning—not where you live or what's parked in your garage. God values the heart more than social status or wealth. One's heart is the true worth of a person, as it defines a person's character (see Luke 21:1–4; Luke 16:15; and Luke 12:15).

A household of lots of stuff is indicative of someone who has an empty place in their life they are attempting to fill—unsuccessfully. It is in our passions, what is in our hearts that reflect our true character and what we value (see Prov. 27:19). Satisfaction does not come from the accumulation of things. This action of collecting is illusory and futile.

I do not deny it is nice to have a few special items on display in one's home. In my later years, I have come to realize that moving from one residence to another can be unpleasant when there are a lot of things to pack. My beliefs and actions have evolved and matured in this regard. I truly believe that something either needs to be an item I use or gives me great pleasure in order to be added to or kept in my home. I wish I had taken up this philosophy much earlier in my life. I wasted a lot of money catering to my wants and desires. I would have had a lot more money to take a well-deserved vacation or donate to a worthy cause. Do you see this waste in your life as well?

We cannot continually maintain being self-promoting or self-indulgent. These are futile tasks with no lasting rewards. In fact, there is tremendous risk in being self-centered. We lose our sensitivity toward the world. Instead, we must refocus on being humble and worthy of God's favor. People around you will take notice and want some of that peace displayed in you (see Eph. 4:17–19).

Greed is indicative of a hardened heart. It cannot hear or understand the Word of God. Such a person is focused on shallow, tactile, and selfish wants because of an unfocused and purposeless life. Put your trust in God and maintain a heavenly focus to create a good foundation for the future benefit of everyone, including yourself. Be content to follow simplicity in living and know that God will provide for what we all truly need.

> True godliness with contentment is itself great wealth.
> After all, we brought nothing with us when we came into

the world, and we can't take anything with us when we leave it. So if we have enough food and clothing, let us be content.

But people who long to be rich fall into temptation and are trapped by many foolish and harmful desires that plunge them into ruin and destruction. For the love of money is the root of all kinds of evil. And some people, craving money, have wandered from the true faith and pierced themselves with many sorrows.

Teach those who are rich in this world not to be proud and not to trust in their money, which is so unreliable. Their trust should be in God, who richly gives us all we need for our enjoyment. Tell them to use their money to do good. They should be rich in good works and generous to those in need, always being ready to share with others. By doing this they will be storing up their treasure as a good foundation for the future so that they may experience true life. (1 Tim. 6:6–10, 17–19 NLT)

Many people make the mistake of interpreting these passages and other ones talking about money as meaning monetary wealth is evil. This is far from the truth. Scripture frequently uses concrete examples of everyday things to make a particular point understandable for everyone. Money is often used in scripture as merely a universal example to illustrate one's true motives. It is attitude and motivation, the focus of our heart's desires that really matters—not how much money we have. Jesus does not ever put down ambition or success. We are charged with being active participants in our lives as well as those lives around us. If some are successful, they typically share in their success, monetarily or otherwise. Jesus justly rewards his faithful and obedient people (see Eccles. 5:19 NLT).

Really, the path your life takes depends on your focus. Are you fleshly or spiritually focused? What awakens you and motivates you into action?

SPIRITUAL RENEWAL

Do not look to worldly, earthly things to find peace, joy, and happiness. These only come from being filled with the Holy Spirit. The old ways of thinking and behaving are worthless and should be discarded. A refreshing newness of life is here and available to you. Accept this heavenly gift. Be revitalized through letting go of the worldly lusts that paralyze (see 1 John 2:15–16). Ask to be filled with the Holy Spirit to help guide you through this worldly maze of material goods. Ask the Holy Spirit to give you all you need to be happy, successful, and productive.

It makes sense that we cannot embrace our heavenly God and worldly goods at the same time. A house divided cannot stand (see Luke 11:17 and Gal. 5:16–21). We have heard that many times. We need our friends and neighbors. But we can do well without some of their misaligned thoughts and behaviors. However important it is to be insulated from the world, we must not be isolated from the world. We need to learn the difference between the self-indulgence and spiritual fulfillment of both ourselves and the people around us. We cannot focus on both. We have appetites for many things. But to be thoroughly satisfied, we need to focus on the spiritual first. The rest will naturally follow (see Eph. 5:17–18).

Let's discuss our physical forms that exist on earth. During our time here, we must be vigilant in the treatment of our bodies. Our body is the temple of the Holy Spirit. Take care of this fragile vessel. Do not defile it. The consequences are often too real and horrendous. Love and respect yourself as God does. He has a plan for your life, and you have the responsibility to be available for whatever he has planned (see 1 Cor. 6:18–20 and 1 Cor. 3:16).

Yes, honor and take care of your earthly vessel. Your body holds your heart and mind, and any defilement can destroy the promise of an eternal future. You are God's temple, and the Holy Spirit must be able to reside there to guide and enlighten you. How else can you grow and mature?

Don't eliminate the possibilities. Success and happiness are at risk of permanent damage (see Gal. 6:7–8 and 2 Tim. 4:3–4).

We need the Holy Spirit to operate within our bodies to reveal the truth; to give us clarity and an understanding of the truth; to keep us focused on the truth. Without a spiritual transformation, humankind is completely inadequate to understand or comprehend the truth found in scripture, including those truths concerning future prophecy. We already tend to hear only those things agreeing with our way of thinking. We become trapped by our earthbound way of rationalization.

The Holy Spirit has been given to us to live wisely in accordance with God's plan. It is up to us to be willing to hear and to learn that which Jesus has taught us. We have a choice of accepting divine destiny or selfish slavery. Is your focus earthly or heavenly? This can ultimately be a life-or-death decision.

> Since you have heard about Jesus and have learned the truth that comes from him, throw off your old sinful nature and your former way of life, which is corrupted by lust and deception. Instead, let the Spirit renew your thoughts and attitudes. Put on your new nature, created to be like God—truly righteous and holy. (Eph. 4:21–24 NLT).

CHRISTLIKE TRANSFORMATION

Live Godly in Christ, for we are transformed into a new creation because of the cross. As faithful followers, we are being conformed to the image of Jesus. We put on his attributes like compassion, forgiveness, humility, gentleness, patience, and, above all, love (see Col. 3:12–14). The Holy Spirit helps us to form and reflect the likeness of Jesus within ourselves and toward others. Live with a humble heart, as we are compelled to be like Christ (see Gal. 5:24 and Rom. 8:29 AMP).

How do I know I am being Christlike? Ask yourself three things: "Am I acting for the right thing, at the right time, for the right reason?" If any one of these is a no, then the answer is no. Fear not though. For as you practice changes, an evolution in thinking and behavior will soon become a natural part of your new character—your transformation. You will begin to notice changes. People around you will take notice. Take great enjoyment and excitement in being the unique person God has always planned for you to be (see Rom. 12:2 NLT).

Remember that our influence on other people is so important. Our behaviors can affect our own walk with Christ as well as that of others. What we think, say, and do is in view of other people. We must always reject every kind of immorality and impurity and set a good example. Christ incarnates himself in us. Therefore, we should follow God's example and walk in the way of his love that exists in our hearts.

> Follow God's example, therefore, as dearly loved children and walk in the way of love, just as Christ loved us and gave himself up for us as a fragrant offering and sacrifice to God.
>
> But among you there must not be even a hint of sexual immorality, or of any kind of impurity, or of greed, because these are improper for God's holy people. Nor should there be obscenity, foolish talk or coarse joking, which are out of place, but rather thanksgiving. For of this you can be sure: No immoral, impure or greedy person—such a person is an idolater—has any inheritance in the kingdom of Christ and of God. (Eph. 5:1–5; see also Titus 2:12 NLT)

When we truly rely on God, we let go of our own burdens and improper behaviors and are finally able to express Christlike behaviors toward others. We must use words and actions of value and edification. We must not be earthly focused but God centered (see 1 Sam. 16:7).

WISDOM AND UNDERSTANDING

Smart people seek out the whys and wherefores of things. If you are uncertain about something, do you not look for answers? Consider that worldly knowledge is often flawed. Take care in what you learn and disseminate to others. We can be confident in the fact that heavenly knowledge is reliable and eternal (see 2 Cor. 1:12).

When we are young and impressionable, we crave learning about the world around us. But as we experience things, there are often painful encounters. These make us more and more hesitant to be open to new learning as we get older. Once bitten, twice shy? Rest assured we are never too old to learn something new. In fact, it's healthy to explore and seek out new knowledge. It can be exciting and rewarding. It increases the likelihood of great things happening for both ourselves and other people. Every time we learn something new, we broaden our understanding of things—both worldly and spiritually. Therefore, we must never refuse to gain wisdom.

Often in the Bible, fear is equal to awe and reverence but not in an earthly sense. It is not based upon judgment or punishment. Rather, this fear is meant to lead us to righteousness and wisdom (see Prov. 1:7). The wisdom that comes from a heavenly focus is revealed by a good and humble life, free of evil and sin.

Be ambitious. God expects and encourages us to be active participants in our lives. Our ambitions need to be centered on living peacefully and supportively of one another. We must avoid bringing chaos into this world. It has enough already without our assistance.

> Who is wise and understanding among you? Let them show it by their good life, by deeds done in the humility that comes from wisdom. But if you harbor bitter envy and selfish ambition in your hearts, do not boast about it or deny the truth. Such "wisdom" does not come down

from heaven but is earthly, unspiritual, demonic. For where you have envy and selfish ambition, there you find disorder and every evil practice.

But the wisdom that comes from heaven is first of all pure; then peace-loving, considerate, submissive, full of mercy and good fruit, impartial and sincere. Peacemakers who sow in peace reap a harvest of righteousness. (James 3:13–18; see also Ps. 111:10 and 1 Pet. 1:14)

Real treasures are found in the wisdom that comes from God. When that wisdom enters your heart, your soul will relish the knowledge that is revealed. The mystery begins to be divulged to you. Feel the safety and security of being surrounded by truth and love (see Prov. 2:1–11 and Job 28 NLT).

$\mathcal{E}$TERNAL FOCUS

Things as we know them in our earthly life will one day pass away. The Word of God never will (see Mark 13:31). Therefore, our lives must not be focused on the temporary, fleshly desires but on the eternal, spiritual life wrapped in truth. The ultimate reality is the difference between salvation and destruction.

Earthly splendor will be rendered meaningless and worthless by death and the coming of God's judgment. We have to want to change our focus and to actively do so. To wait until we are suffering makes the path much more difficult (see Luke 16:19–29 and 2 Pet. 3:10–13).

It wasn't so long ago that you were mired in that old stagnant life of sin. You let the world, which doesn't know the first thing about living, tell you how to live. You filled your lungs with polluted unbelief, and then exhaled disobedience. We all did it, all of us doing what we felt

like doing, when we felt like doing it, all of us in the same
boat. It's a wonder God didn't lose his temper and do away
with the whole lot of us. Instead, immense in mercy and
with an incredible love, he embraced us. He took our sin-
dead lives and made us alive in Christ. (Eph. 2:1–5 MSG)

There is an everlasting quality of God in contrast to the frailty of
humankind. Humans have but a momentary existence on earth. God has
an eternity in heaven. He is clear in his promise to us to share eternity
with him, to share in his divine nature (see 2 Pet. 1:4 NLT and 2 Cor.
7:1). It is a freely offered gift to every one of us. We cannot ignore this.
We cannot be self-centered, materialistic, or earthly bound in our focus
or actions. Material goods are temporary, and the spiritual are eternal. We
have a choice to make.

The apostle Paul regularly encourages us to develop a transforming,
eternal focus. He reminds us that the value of our lives is not determined by
what we have but by how we live. He demonstrated to us that surrounding
ourselves with other Christians can help us to focus on living as examples
of righteous behavior. Together we can encourage and edify one another
in this life, to prosper in everything we do. Together we can await the
chosen time when we can leave these corporal bodies behind and share in
the mysteries of God.

Join together in following my example, brothers and
sisters, and just as you have us as a model, keep your
eyes on those who live as we do. For, as I have often told
you before and now tell you again even with tears, many
live as enemies of the cross of Christ. Their destiny is
destruction, their god is their stomach, and their glory is
in their shame. Their mind is set on earthly things. But
our citizenship is in heaven. And we eagerly await a Savior
from there, the Lord Jesus Christ, who, by the power that
enables him to bring everything under his control, will

transform our lowly bodies so that they will be like his glorious body. (Phil. 3:17–21)

Let go of your earthly perspectives. Transform your habits. Move away from your patterns that have created a temporary comfort zone. As you grow in faith, do not compromise your new boundaries. Stick to them. You are an active participant in developing and maturing your character. Make good, wise choices (see Luke 21:34–36).

Take a step toward eternity in heaven and let go of your earthbound, fleshly desires. Those are not really required on earth anyway! Journey from the familiar to the unknown. Take a leap of faith. Change can be frightening or exciting, depending on one's frame of mind. You can be a negative or positive thinker. Which are you most of the time? A new way of thinking is here. A new world view is available here and now.

Attitude is the compass by which we traverse this life on earth. Circumstances we encounter in daily living can often infiltrate and influence our attitudes. We gain life's strength or weakness from our attitudes. Through a Christ-based life, we are provided opportunities to maintain positive attitudes and hence a positive life of satisfaction and fulfillment. Are you the tree planted by the water who grows and flourishes and produces much fruit (see Jer. 17:5–8)?

Sending out our positive energy into God's universe is a perfect way to honor the glory and magnificence of all God has created and done for us. We tend to reap what we sow. Now might be the time to become a positive person (see Phil. 4:8).

Focus on Reconciliation

God has unconditional love for us. It is genuine and everlasting. Nothing on earth can measure up the same (see Luke 12:21). It's time to focus not on earthly things but to seek out God, reaching for him in heavenly places with our hearts and minds. He created everything for us. And he is ready for a personal relationship with each and every one of us. He invites us to seek him and to call to him. He is right there waiting. We have the choice to accept or decline this invitation (see Acts 17:26–27 and Col. 3:1–2 NLT).

The apostle Paul reminds us of the importance of centering our focus on a relationship with God. It doesn't matter what your sins are. We all sin and are in the same place. We are all equal in the eyes of God. We are offered a fresh start through the forgiveness of our sins. We are all invited to be forgiven and to reestablish a close relationship with him. We all have this same offer, to gain a new and better life.

> Our firm decision is to work from this focused center: One man died for everyone. That puts everyone in the same boat. He included everyone in his death so that everyone could also be included in his life, a resurrection life, a far better life than people ever lived on their own.
>
> Because of this decision we don't evaluate people by what they have or how they look. We looked at the Messiah that way once and got it all wrong, as you know. We certainly don't look at him that way anymore. Now we look inside, and what we see is that anyone united with the Messiah gets a fresh start, is created new. The old life is gone; a new life burgeons! Look at it! All this comes from the God who settled the relationship between us and him, and then called us to settle our relationships with each other. God put the world square with himself through the Messiah, giving the world a fresh start by offering forgiveness of sins. God has given us the task of telling everyone what he is doing. We're Christ's representatives. God uses us to persuade men and women to drop their differences and enter into God's work of making things right between them. We're speaking for Christ himself now: Become

friends with God; he's already a friend with you. (2 Cor. 5:14–20 MSG)

Life on earth is fast drawing to a close. Do not be caught unaware of this or by losing your focus in earthly desires. It's time to focus on God, who promises an eternity of happiness and security (see Rom. 13:11–14). It's not too late to change the focus of your life. But it soon will be. Your family in Christ awaits you in your new life and to share with you your new rewards. Failure is merely hope abandoned!

We're not giving up. How could we! Even though on the outside it often looks like things are falling apart on us, on the inside, where God is making new life, not a day goes by without his unfolding grace. These hard times are small potatoes compared to the coming good times, the lavish celebration prepared for us. There's far more here than meets the eye. The things we see now are here today, gone tomorrow. But the things we can't see now will last forever. (2 Cor. 4:16–18 MSG)

Grace and Salvation

GRACE IS GOD'S good favor—his pleasure and kindness extended toward humankind. It is manifested in God's gift of salvation, which is unearned and unmerited mercy given to sinners. This is a free gift offered to every single one of us. We are all sinners who require someone to step in and grant us an opportunity for salvation. Redemption and absolution only come from receiving God's grace, which then releases us from the guilt created by and punishment demanded for our sins. With God's salvation comes a blessing of gifts we freely enjoy in life and can only receive from God.

> He has saved us and called us to a holy life—not because of anything we have done but because of his own purpose and grace. This grace was given us in Christ Jesus before the beginning of time, but it has now been revealed through the appearing of our Savior, Christ Jesus, who has destroyed death and has brought life and immortality to light through the gospel. (2 Tim. 1:9–10)

Let us begin by outlining a few of the key concepts and what they mean for us. Grace is freely getting things we don't deserve but need. Mercy is not being punished for our sins as we deserve to be. Confession of our sins means we acknowledge, declare, and admit our faults and wrongs. Repentance is our own controlling power of free will. In this, we have the ability to recognize sin and turn away from it, to transform the way we say and do things. It is within our repentance that we find the promise of God's love and mercy and his free gift of salvation through his good grace. God's salvation is his controlling power rescuing us from the effects of our bad choices or sins, namely punishment and death.

It was John the Baptist, cousin of Jesus, who spent much of his life announcing the coming of the gift of grace into the world. This gift was to come through Jesus Christ. The apostle Luke tells us John provided the knowledge of what we need to do to receive the gift and what this would mean for us now and in the long run (see Luke 1:76–78).

SALVATION FOR ALL

God offers salvation to everyone. He desires for every single one of us to experience his redeeming grace. Salvation is given to all who come to faith in Jesus, whether a long-term believer or a death bed convert. We can never judge another's conversion or the deserving of God's grace. For only God knows the truth of what is in a person's heart. It is enough for us to know that it is a free gift from God for all people. And thankfully, God is patient, letting each of us come to repentance in our own time. His desire is for everyone to repent and receive his free gift of salvation. It would not be free otherwise. We must decide that this is what we want. Nobody else can make this decision for us (see 2 Pet. 3:8–9 NLT).

> He wants not only us but everyone saved, you know, everyone to get to know the truth we've learned: that there's one God and only one, and one Priest-Mediator between God and us—Jesus, who offered himself in exchange for everyone held captive by sin, to set them all free. Eventually the news is going to get out. This and this

only has been my appointed work: getting this news to
those who have never heard of God, and explaining how
it works by simple faith and plain truth. (1 Tim. 2:4–7
MSG; see also Acts 2:21; Acts 4:12; and Rom. 10:9, 13)

It is not just God's chosen people, the Jews, who are eligible to receive
the gift of salvation. Jesus brought this promised gift to all people. We all
are offered this free gift. Even the Gentiles have been chosen to receive it.
Yes, salvation is offered to everyone, both Jew and Gentile. For we all have
sinned. All are equal in our sinning. All are in need of God's redemptive
grace (see Rom. 11:11 NLT and Jer. 33:14–16 NLT).

God made a personal sacrifice for our salvation, to win our freedom
from the consequences of our sins. There is no possible way any of us can
pay adequately for our sins. Jesus did this for us. The one who knew no
sin took upon himself all the punishments we all deserve for all our sins.
God revealed his good and loving character in granting us mercy—to take
the deserved punishment away from us and place it on his Son, Jesus (see
Eph. 1:6–7 NLT).

Salvation comes through the cross. The cross was God's remedy for our
redemption and reconciliation. It took a physical death to give us spiritual
life. The tremendous power of God is seen in that sacrificial gift, in the
message of the cross (see 1 Cor. 1:18).

There is an important aspect to God's gift of grace, to any gift really.
The true measure or value of any gift is not in how much is given but rather
in how much there was to give. It's the intention or heart of the giver that
is of importance and gives the giving of the gift its value. God clearly loves
us tremendously, as is demonstrated in his deeply personal and sacrificial
gift—that of his Son's brutal death and resurrection to rescue and reunite
with every single one of us (see Ps. 91:14–16 and Heb. 2:3–4).

$\mathcal{W}$ORKS

God owes us nothing. We owe him everything. Because, to begin with, everything comes from God in the first place. Grace is not an entitlement. It is never earned and is not to be expected from God. It is a free gift. It is very important you understand this. Grace is not the result of works but a free gift from God. This is the definition of a gift. It's freely given. And we are chosen by God to receive his free gift of grace.

> God saved you by his grace when you believed. And you can't take credit for this; it is a gift from God. Salvation is not a reward for the good things we have done, so none of us can boast about it. (Eph. 2:8–9 NLT; see also Rom. 11:35–36 and Rom. 11:6)

The apostle Paul often wrote of our salvation. He has been quite clear that it is received by grace through our faith in Jesus Christ (see Eph. 1:13–14 and Isa. 65:17–25). And as children of God, we become heirs to all he freely offers. Paul was very specific that God's gift of grace is never ever granted by our works—nothing we can do. Nobody will ever get to heaven by their good works. It cannot be earned or owed to us. It is not based upon any merit system. It is a free and just gift of redemption and a promise of a close, personal relationship with God. The wonderful thing is that we receive eternal life as the outcome of our reconciliation with God (see Titus 3:4–7; Rom. 3:28; and Acts 15:11).

It is only through the transformation of our hearts and minds that we begin to do good works. We become filled with the Holy Spirit and cannot help but want and need to do good works. This is a demonstration of our new nature. We are transformed from selfish to selfless. The floodgates of real joy open, and we are renewed. We are now free to become the person we always wanted to be—the person God had planned from the start (see Ps. 40:8 and 2 Cor. 1:12).

With this new character developing within us, God will be seen in us. It is our responsibility to hold up the light of God's Word so others can see what he has done for us and what he can do for them. Reveal the reason for your joy and hope. Let people see your good works reflecting the glory of God (see Matt. 5:16 NLT).

*O*BEDIENCE

God's gift of salvation creates a relationship and a covenant with humankind that carries with them certain expectations and demands. There has always been a plan and a purpose, and we must be obedient in actively fulfilling our role with respect and reverence. He has expectations that we will be active participants in life. We are to not only transform our lives but to facilitate in transforming the lives of others, to take on an active role in the community (see Luke 12:48b).

God counsels us in faithful obedience. In this we can be confident and depend on him. He has sent the Holy Spirit to help us every step of the way. The Holy Spirit fills us with the desire and gives us the abilities to be fruitful (see Phil. 2:12–13 NLT).

Every loving relationship with God rests upon his grace and generosity. God's blessings flow to us and through us. These blessings must be shared with other people. We wrongly assume the harder we work, the greater our reward. It is not a self-effort merit system at work here but our responsiveness to God's Word that counts. God rewards us not on the basis of how much we do but rather how fruitfully we respond to his will. What and how much is done based upon his directions defines our fruitfulness and not our reward. Salvation never comes from our works but from obedience to God. We must remain obedient to God's promises and all the great things flowing from them.

JUDGMENT AND REDEMPTION

Salvation is redemption from our sinful actions occurring while we are in this earthly place. Redemption brings with it not simply absolution for our sins but a recovery of our estranged relationship with God. Sin was brought into this world through the actions of Adam. The punishment for sin, which is death, was borne out of this first sin.

God passed judgment following the one sin of Adam and brought condemnation through death. The gift of grace has followed after the many trespasses of humankind since then. It brought redemption through the death and resurrection of Jesus and justification for the restoration of eternal life (see Rom. 5:12–19; Rom. 6:23; and Gen. 3).

Jesus paid the ultimate price for our sins. Through this, we are justified and have been given eternal life instead of death. The only way out of the cycle of sin and death is through God's free gift of grace. The result is the restoration of eternal life and a renewed relationship with God.

At the end of life on earth, the Bible states a final judgment will precede our gift of eternal life. Yes, unfortunately, we all must face a final judgment upon Christ's return (see 2 Cor. 5:10). Take heart though! We have an advocate in Jesus Christ. He will stand with us before God at the final judgment. If your heart has been faithful and obedient to God, then there is no fear of condemnation (see Rom. 8:1). Be confident in your renewed, productive life. Trust in God's renewed relationship with you.

The apostle Paul reminds us of his own wretched past of murderous sin and persecution. It was by the grace of God that his heart was transformed. He repented and changed the way he thought and behaved. He became one of the greatest apostles of Jesus and represents one of the most relatable stories of redemption (see 1 Cor. 15:9–10).

Release your fears and trust in God's promises. It is through our struggles and suffering in this world and our actively seeking God that we can emerge into an experience of God's loving compassion and redemptive mercy. We can find rest in God through his grace. We will receive redemption and protection in the final judgement. Justification can be ours. Confidence is ours (see Heb. 4:16; Matt. 11:28; 2 Cor. 7:10; James 5:11; and Isa. 30:19 MSG).

THE LAW OF GRACE AND RIGHTEOUSNESS

God loves us as a parent does his child. He will never shame us. Never. But he does offer us a way to change our lives, to make our lives better. No matter what horrible things our past holds, through God's free gift of grace, we can move forward into a new, justifiable life. We can become worthy of salvation and be treated as righteous individuals. Righteousness, doing what is right and good, gives us a freedom from guilt and sin. It comes only through our faith and God's grace (see Rom. 3:21–25).

We are no longer governed by the enslaving laws of Moses but by the freeing grace of God. This law of grace is the difference between death and life, slavery and freedom. It is the pathway to truth and a glimpse into the mysteries of God (see John 1:17; Eph. 4:7; and Gal. 5:4).

> Count yourselves dead to sin but alive to God in Christ Jesus. Therefore do not let sin reign in your mortal body so that you obey its evil desires. Do not offer any part of yourself to sin as an instrument of wickedness, but rather offer yourselves to God as those who have been brought from death to life; and offer every part of yourself to him as an instrument of righteousness. For sin shall no longer be your master, because you are not under the law, but under grace. (Rom. 6:11–14)

What is the bottom line of our salvation? God has planned the creation of a new heaven and new earth as a home for the righteous (see Rev. 21:1–4). By truly accepting God into our lives, we are made righteous. A righteous person is one who leads a morally just life that is pleasing to God.

This is not always easy for most of us to do because of our surroundings, either places or people or both. These often can make it difficult for us to behave righteously. We have choices in all areas of our lives. Make the right choices and make the right changes to make your salvation possible (see Titus 2:11–12).

Change can be seen as a scary thing to face, especially alone. Surround yourself with other Christians, and you will change your outlook and your life. Elation, happiness, and peace are some of the descriptors I've heard people use to define how they feel through the redemptive power of Christ. I pray you will find pure excitement through your journey into a new realm of existence.

Be holy in your new life. Maintain a just and moral character. Be dedicated to living a life focused on righteousness and fruitfulness and become worthy of salvation. It is how we live our lives from now until the time of Christ's return that is important, especially considering nobody knows when this will occur.

> The LORD has sent this message to every land: "Tell the people of Israel, 'Look, your Savior is coming. See, he brings his reward with him as he comes.'" (Isa. 62:11 NLT); see also 1 Pet. 1:13; 2 Pet. 3:10–11, 13)

Forgiveness and Love

GOD HAS A desire to have a close, loving relationship with us. But in order to accomplish this, we need to be reconciled with God. In other words, we need to experience forgiveness and redemption for our sinful behaviors. Since before creation, there has been a grand plan concerning our forgiveness and redemption and the ultimate goal of reconciliation with God.

Redemption involves a repayment and a recovery. Redemption means a saving from error, evil, or sin—in other words, bad or immoral behaviors. It is an act of making something more acceptable and worthy of recovery in exchange for payment or forgiveness of a debt. In our case, the debt refers to our getting away with our criminal behaviors. Someone is required to pay that debt so we can be recovered and reconciled with God. It was Jesus Christ who paid the brutal price for each of our sins—with his own blood, all so that we could return to a loving relationship with God (see Eph. 1:7 and Heb. 9:22).

Understand that God cannot have anything to do with sin. So, we must be cleansed of our sins to be able to have any relationship with God. This involves two actions. The first act of redemption has already been completed by God. God established a path to redemption through the sacrificial blood of Jesus. We are washed clean and pure in his blood. In this way, he has cleansed us of all disease, past, present, and future.

We know we are not perfect on our own. None of us are. We will all be sinful from time to time. It's in our nature since Adam. Jesus was sent to us for this very reason. He was sent to show us the path, the way back to righteous behavior and God. He came to heal us, to repair our relationships, and to teach us how to live righteously with God and one another.

> Jesus said, "It is not the healthy who need a doctor, but the sick. But go and learn what this means: 'I desire mercy, not sacrifice.' For I have not come to call the righteous, but sinners." (Matt. 9:12–13)

The second act of redemption requires us to confess and repent of our sinful ways in both our thoughts and behaviors. To confess means to admit or be truthful about our sins. To repent means to turn around, to change our sinful ways. Confession is pointless if we do not repent and change our ways. The sincerity of our confession will determine our success in changing our ways—the way we think and act.

Humility is crucial to confessing and repenting of our past sinful words, thoughts, and deeds. Each of us must become humble, free from earthbound arrogance or self-centered pride, and open our hearts and minds to what God offers. This selfless humility is a source of freedom for us and opens up the opportunity to experience a relationship with God. We must demonstrate our sorrow for our sins and reveal a change of heart by a change in our behaviors. This is proof of repentance (see 1 John 1:8–9).

As we grow in our understanding and in our practice of living a refreshed life, the Holy Spirit that Jesus Christ places within us is always available to help as a guide along the right path. It is not always an easy road to traverse. Righteousness takes practice to perfect within our daily repertoire. It does not happen overnight.

Forgiveness means to release someone from the bonds of judgment and punishment. It is true freedom. We can be confident that when each of us receives Jesus in sincere faith, the forgiveness that comes from God is a one-time event. Once you ask God into your life, the Holy Spirit can be felt, and you will know you are forgiven. And, from that moment forward, it is important that you continue to confess, ask for, and receive his ongoing forgiveness. This is what we do to maintain a close relationship with God, our father. He is there to help us in our daily struggles and to grow and mature.

> I need something more! For if I know the law but still can't keep it, and if the power of sin within me keeps sabotaging my best intentions, I obviously need help! I realize that I don't have what it takes. I can will it, but I can't do it. I decide to do good, but I don't really do it; I decide not to do bad, but then I do it anyway. My decisions, such as they are, don't result in actions. Something has gone wrong deep within me and gets the better of me every time.
>
> It happens so regularly that it's predictable. The moment I decide to do good, sin is there to trip me up. I truly delight in God's commands, but it's pretty obvious that not all of me joins in that delight. Parts of me covertly rebel, and just when I least expect it, they take charge.
>
> I've tried everything and nothing helps. I'm at the end of my rope. Is there no one who can do anything for me? Isn't that the real question?
>
> The answer, thank God, is that Jesus Christ can and does. He acted to set things right in this life of contradictions where I want to serve God with all my heart and mind, but am pulled by the influence of sin to do something totally different. (Rom. 7:17–25 MSG; see also Acts 10:43 and Ps. 130:1–8)

All too often, each of us has been at that tormenting place, facing our proclivity to sin. Life is not without its difficulties. Don't stop asking for help from the Holy Spirit and from fellow Christian travelers! Life has way too many obstacles to go it alone. This journey is meant to be shared not only with God but with fellow Christians.

Being a Christian does not make a perfect or flawless life. It takes a constant process of confession, prayer, and forgiveness to improve life. Learning and maturing day by day will get you there.

It is a blessing to know God has determined we are worthy of forgiveness and redemption. Remember he decided this before creation. It was in his plan. The ultimate choice is ours to accept or decline the invitation to be reconciled with God. A close personal relationship with God for an eternity is so exceptionally worth striving for. And how wonderful to have the chance to become the person you so want to be right now (see Ezek. 18:21–22 NLT and Ps. 32:1–2).

To sum it up, forgiveness takes one action from God: the gift of grace. Reconciliation requires two actions from us: confession and repentance. We need to humbly admit to our sins and change our problematic thoughts and behaviors related to our sinning. The first step is that we must own our sins. Other people must own theirs. Then we become ready to repent and be reconciled to God. It's that easy. God wants a relationship with each one of us and makes the path simple. Keep your sights looking forward down the path toward a better, more positive life. Refuse to look back. Change is exciting and productive (see Isa. 43:16, 18–19).

RECONCILIATION WITH OTHERS

Jesus came to reconcile us not only to our heavenly Father but also to one another. True worship of God is contingent upon our reconciliation with other people. Mend your wounds. Don't let them consume or define your very essence. You are in control of how you feel and what you do (see Matt. 6:14–15; Matt. 5:24; and Ps. 86:5).

Forgiveness must come first—our forgiveness from God and our forgiveness from and for other people. Forgiveness with other people is twofold. Our own actions require forgiveness from others, and other people's actions require forgiveness from us. Forgiveness opens the many doors to repairing or amicably ending relationships. There is tremendous power in forgiveness. Forgiveness frees us and awakens the love in us. It awakens our love for God as proof of his forgiveness. A grateful heart is available to hear the voice of God. A forgiving heart opens up the possibility of new and renewed relationships with others (see Eph. 4:32 and Matt. 3:8).

Yes, sometimes forgiving someone of a crime against us is not an easy task. There are indeed some things too horrific and painful for us to handle, let alone forgive. But we can choose to become a slave to the anger and hurt, or we can choose to let it go. It does not mean we forget an injurious offense. It does mean we can refuse to be held a prisoner by it. Deny the power someone has over your life's happiness.

We have been given God's gift of free will—to choose to be in control of our own lives, our feelings, beliefs, and actions. Don't give up that control to someone else. It's your life. You choose the direction and how you want to get to a place of peace and success.

Reconciliation with others is important. A good heart is demonstrated in our behaviors and attitudes toward other people. Know that our behaviors are contagious! Our actions directly affect or infect society. Real societal change can be accomplished through our positive attitudes. Something as simple as a smile or acknowledging another person in a positive way goes a long way to making changes in lives.

Just think about it. When someone takes a bite of something and smiles, it makes us smile. Then they tilt their face skyward and hum a pleasant sound ... Well, it has the ability to make our own mouth water, and we want a piece of whatever that was. Where did that feeling of joy and happiness come from? It's the same in the joyous feeling of hope we get from a relationship with God. Our simple acts revealing our joy have the power to make someone else want what we have.

Avoid judging others. There is no room for love in judging others. It is not your place either. We are called to edify (instruct and improve) people with kindness, not to rudely condemn them. The tendency is to reap what we sow. Are there flowers or weeds in your garden? You have the power of choice (see Luke 6:37).

Along those same lines, revenge is an attitude based on the judgment, valid or not, that someone has acted against your best interest. Work through it to lose the intense feelings and become forgiving. Again, this does not mean you have to become forgetful. But the past has passed. Let it go and focus on better things for the present and a much-improved future. This is what adults call learning to be bigger than the transgression or the transgressor (see Lev. 19:18).

THE ONE EXCEPTION TO FORGIVENESS

There is only one sin that will never be forgiven by God: blasphemy confined to speech defamatory of the Holy Spirit. Whoever speaks abusively against or maliciously misrepresents the Holy Spirit can never receive forgiveness. They are guilty of and in the grasp of an everlasting trespass, facing eternal consequences. Intent is key, as it is the hardening of the heart against salvation that will bring eternal punishment. The heart is the motivator and hence defines a person's character.

One may initially reject Christianity or aspects of it out of ignorance. But to step out on a limb and cut the lifeline God sends out to reestablish a relationship with you is eternal suicide. My dear Tutu used to say, "You just don't cut off your nose to spite your face." It is quite illogical to reject something when you don't fully comprehend it. Knowledge is the key to understanding. One cannot plead ignorance in front of a judge.

> "There's nothing done or said that can't be forgiven. But if you deliberately persist in your slanders against God's Spirit, you are repudiating the very One who forgives. If you reject the Son of Man out of some misunderstanding, the Holy Spirit can forgive you, but when you reject the Holy Spirit, you're sawing off the branch on which you're sitting, severing by your own perversity all connection with the One who forgives." (Matt. 12:31–32 MSG; see also Luke 12:8–10 and Mark 3:28–29)

The New Law of Love

Owing a debt or requiring punishment for our sinful crimes only exists under the old law. We are no longer under the old covenant laws. The death and resurrection of Jesus Christ ended the old law. The debt for our sins has been paid, and forgiveness is granted within the new covenant law of love. No, our sins can never be undone, but they can be rendered powerless by God's forgiveness. Forgiveness is borne out of love—the love commanded by the new covenant.

Sins cannot exist in someone with a pure, loving heart. None of the original commandment laws can be broken by a person who has only love in their heart. This is not an easy task for us though. We have so much practice being sinners. Don't be anxious though. Good things also take time to practice and to perfect. You can and will get there. God is patient, so you should be as well (see Rom. 13:8–10; Matt. 22:37–40; Mark 12:28–31 NLT; Deut. 6:4–5; and Luke 10:25–27).

Love stems from our freedom from the old law and blossoms through the new law given by God through Jesus. There are great rewards in following this new law. This new covenant law allows us to be saved from eternal punishment, to be secured in our promised place in heaven, and to honor God with productive and fruitful lives.

The commandments to love God with our whole heart, soul, and mind and to love one another as Jesus demonstrated sum up the entire law for Christians and for humankind. The importance to Christianity of this new covenant command is clearly seen by its unceasing repetition throughout the New Testament. We are now free from an immoral past, to experience a marvelous future and to humbly serve one another in love (see Gal. 5:13–14; John 13:34; and John 15:12).

$\mathcal{W}$HAT IS LOVE?

Dear friends, let us love one another, for love comes from God. Everyone who loves has been born of God and knows God. Whoever does not love does not know God, because God is love. This is how God showed his love among us: He sent his one and only Son into the world that we might live through him. This is love: not that we loved God, but that he loved us and sent his Son as an atoning sacrifice for our sins. Dear friends, since God so loved us, we also ought to love one another. No one has ever seen God; but if we love one another, God lives in us and his love is made complete in us.

And so we know and rely on the love God has for us.

God is love. Whoever lives in love lives in God, and God in them. This is how love is made complete among us so that we will have confidence on the day of judgment: In this world we are like Jesus. There is no fear in love. But perfect love drives out fear, because fear has to do with punishment. The one who fears is not made perfect in love. We love because he first loved us. (1 John 4:7–12, 16–19)

This is a beautiful passage from 1 John that perfectly sums up the definition of love. God is love. And from God, we learned how to love. It was God who first loved us and taught us what love is. He taught us the fullest extent of how to love. In fact, his love for us is so great that he made it possible for us to reestablish a relationship with him. He chose to demonstrate the depth of his love by paying the ultimate price for a relationship with us. God sent his only Son to take the repayment of our debt of sin upon himself—a brutal beating and then hanging until death upon the cross. There is no greater love than this (see John 3:16; Rom. 5:8; 1 John 3:16; and John 15:13).

The Greek translation of the Bible reveals that there are actually four types of love in scripture. Agape love is the highest type of love and is selfless, sacrificial, and unconditional (see Zavada 2019). Agape love is not a feeling but a choice, a chosen love. God gave to us first in everything. We are only able to love because God first loved us. For me, this is the greatest gift any of us has received or could ever offer to anyone else. There is such power in agape love. God's love is the wellspring of all life—of all that has come into existence. God's love is constant and never fails. God's love endures forever (see Jer. 31:3 AMP and Jer. 33:11).

LOVE EMPOWERS AND EQUIPS

Love is the only way to happiness and a satisfying, productive life. We all must be rooted and grounded in love. It is then that we can begin to understand the love God has for us. Love is power. Love is knowledge outward bound. This is my favorite way of looking at love. The depth and fullness that one feels from true love bursts outward from inside. It is infectious and motivational. Find that spark of love within yourself, for yourself. It will grow and expand, empowering you, and spread to those around you (see Eph. 3:17–19).

Love is what makes us able to understand and embrace the Lord's teachings and creates the desire to share it with others. It's important to not only be self-aware but to also maintain an awareness of others. It gives a personal insight into the reality around you. This leads to a growing awareness of not only what you can do for yourself but also what you can do and be for others. With a growing awareness, you will be able to spot those instances where you can be of assistance and help others. Ask yourself, "What can I do to facilitate happiness and success in the lives of others?" Become a positive influence. Nobody can stifle a smile when someone is happy. A smile is contagious. It has the power to change the trajectory of lives (see Phil. 1:9–10).

Love is a spectacular feeling. It is best when shared. We are called to love God and to love others. Loving our neighbors is a reflection of our loving God first. Loving God inspires and equips us for service to others. This is not always an easy thing to do. Sometimes it's difficult to love others. Sometimes it involves a sacrifice. But if we can focus on loving God first, it becomes a natural progression and easier to do (see 1 John 4:20–21).

Love was a gift from God. It becomes a part of us, our very being, through our belief in and relationship with Christ. This ever growing and expanding love within us gives the power to emulate Christlike behavior and attitudes, such as compassion, forgiveness, generosity, and so on. "Freely you have received from God, so freely give to others." I grew up hearing this. It warms my heart to share it with you. We must be generous to all and follow the example of Jesus. Focus on Godly living.

> Therefore if you have any encouragement from being united with Christ, if any comfort from his love, if any common sharing in the Spirit, if any tenderness and compassion, then make my joy complete by being like-minded, having the same love, being one in spirit and of one mind. Do nothing out of selfish ambition or vain

conceit. Rather, in humility value others above yourselves, not looking to your own interests but each of you to the interests of the others. (Phil. 2:1–4; see also 1 Cor. 16:13–14; Matt. 10:8; and Rom. 12:9–10)

Jesus calls us to make active, unselfish use of our compassion for others. There is little value in any sacrifice we make or offer to someone if it does not begin in an unselfish heart. It is in our unselfish actions toward others that we demonstrate God's love within us. Remember the old adage that actions speak louder than words? Our character is revealed by how we demonstrate our love, not merely through our words. Actions motivated with integrity will speak volumes and accomplish a lot (see 1 John 3:18).

Our lives become nothing of practical importance, unable to gain much of substantial value, without love. You can be sure a life without love is empty, fraught with misery, and unfulfilling. The first step in receiving love from others is to take the chance and reach out and share some love.

If I speak with human eloquence and angelic ecstasy but don't love, I'm nothing but the creaking of a rusty gate.

If I speak God's Word with power, revealing all his mysteries and making everything plain as day, and if I have faith that says to a mountain, "Jump," and it jumps, but I don't love, I'm nothing.

If I give everything I own to the poor and even go to the stake to be burned as a martyr, but I don't love, I've gotten nowhere. So, no matter what I say, what I believe, and what I do, I'm bankrupt without love.

Love never gives up. Love cares more for others than for self. Love doesn't want what it doesn't have. Love doesn't strut, Doesn't have a swelled head, Doesn't force itself on others, Isn't always "me first," Doesn't fly off the handle,

Doesn't keep score of the sins of others, Doesn't revel when others grovel, Takes pleasure in the flowering of truth, Puts up with anything, Trusts God always, Always looks for the best, Never looks back, But keeps going to the end. (1 Cor. 13:1–7 MSG)

In the last paragraph above, from 1 Corinthians, replace the word *love* with your name. How does it stack up? Now try saying that passage using the name of Jesus. Amazing isn't it? What were the differences between using your name and that of Jesus? What can you do to make them more in line with each other?

Love must be an action verb. We are called to love one another with genuine affection and to take delight in honoring and encouraging one another. A smile from someone you help can bring a lifetime of joy to both of you. That smile can break down a wall or forge a friendship, which will not only pay you back but also spread far and wide to others. It solidifies your character and establishes how others will perceive you in the future (see 1 Tim. 1:5; 1 Pet. 1:22; and 1 John 3:11).

Love's Promises

Nothing can separate us from the love of God. His love is enduring and unchanging. It can never be shaken or taken. God is faithful in his unconditional love toward us (see Ps. 33:4–5). There is no person or anything anywhere that can stop God from loving each one of us. This is guaranteed. On this you can rely. He awaits the moment when you step forward and ask him into your life (see Rom. 8:37–39; Ps. 136:1, 26; Ps. 107:43; and Isa. 54:10).

Faithful obedience to Jesus demonstrates our love for God. It brings with it a guarantee of a meaningful, personal relationship with him. It is your choice to make. No one can make it for you (see John 14:21 NLT; Ps. 103:8–12; and Eph. 5:1–2). Life is so much better with God's unconditional love paving the way. It fills us with security and motivation, peace and action.

The chaos in the world continually attacks our stability both mentally and physically. Love brings peace. Let go of the earthly desires and focus on the higher, heavenly goals. When the Holy Spirit fills your heart, you will understand the power of love and be motivated into action. God has so much to give to those who love and pursue righteousness. Through them, we gain honor, prosperity, and a life worth living (see Prov. 21:21; 1 Cor. 2:9; Prov. 11:25; and Rom. 8:28).

We are made perfect in God's love. Our sins and transgressions are forgiven through the love of God. Accepting God's love frees us from the entrapments of worldly fears. Remember 1 John 4:18, "There is no fear in love." Love binds everything together in perfect unity.

> Therefore, as God's chosen people, holy and dearly loved, clothe yourselves with compassion, kindness, humility, gentleness and patience. Bear with each other and forgive one another if any of you has a grievance against someone. Forgive as the Lord forgave you. And over all these virtues put on love, which binds them all together in perfect unity. (Col. 3:12–14)

Our journey into Christianity is not cut and dry. There are walls to break down within our hearts and minds, which can open us up to understanding and experiencing love. Our ability to give and receive love gives us permission to give and receive forgiveness. Pray for enlightenment and clarity from the Holy Spirit, for love truly is the key to everything.

> We don't yet see things clearly. We're squinting in a fog, peering through a mist. But it won't be long before the weather clears and the sun shines bright! We'll see it all then, see it all as clearly as God sees us, knowing him directly just as he knows us! But for right now, until

that completeness, we have three things to do to lead us toward that consummation: Trust steadily in God, hope unswervingly, love extravagantly. And the best of the three is love. (1 Cor. 13:12–13 MSG)

Faith and Trust

THE ESSENCE OF faith is the trust borne out of the love we have for God. And it is our faith in God's unconditional love that gives us the hope to work through the trials and tribulations encountered in this earthly life. It is through the perseverance of our faith that our good character is developed and we find hope, joy, and peace.

We must trust in God's grace and truth. Our faith is the expression of our confidence, our trust in God's promises of his gift of grace and the truth of everything he reveals to us. This includes the ultimate reward of eternal life with him in heaven (see Rom. 5:1–2 and Rom. 15:13 NLT).

Faith Demonstrated in the Bible

God is huge. We cannot attempt to bring him down to our level of understanding. Rather, we need to halt our earthly centered thinking and stretch toward faithfully accepting the omnipotence of God. Opportunity comes from trusting God, from having faith in God. We must always maintain trust and faith in God and his plan. History has continually demonstrated the results (see Rom. 4:18–21 and Gen. 17:17).

Faith is not something to be questioned but rather something to be lived. In the Old Testament, we read about the many histories of the heirs of God's promises and the faith demonstrated by them. Yet the personal receipt of a final reward was always absent. This is because God has a plan for humankind's ultimate rewards. This plan was set in motion before creation and fulfilled by the sacrifice of Jesus on the cross. There could be no ultimate rewards without the new covenant promises that came through Jesus. The New Testament reveals that it is only from faith in Jesus Christ that humankind will reap the benefits of God's ultimate rewards. He has promised us an eternal life with him and all the blessings that come with it (see Heb. 11:39–40).

> Now faith is confidence in what we hope for and assurance
> about what we do not see. This is what the ancients were
> commended for. (Heb. 11:1–2)

In the Hebrews, chapter 11, verses, we learn that so many generations of individuals, both men and women, demonstrated their faith and trust in God. They held in their hearts the knowledge and the confidence that God's ultimate rewards were something worth living and dying for (see Heb. 11:13–16).

Jesus demonstrated to his disciples the importance of an active faith (see Matt. 8:23–26 and Mark 4:35–40). Yet even his disciples experienced wavering faith at times. So let me ask you, when Christ returns, will he find persistence of faith in us as his new disciples? Are you a concrete thinker who requires physical proofs? (see 2 Cor. 5:7).

ℱAITH DEMONSTRATED TODAY

A Christian life is not just a changed life but an exchanged life. As we place our faith and trust in Jesus, so he also puts his faith and trust in us to think and act appropriately and righteously. This can be tough. Take heart though, as we are not on this journey alone. Jesus is "the pioneer and perfecter" of our faith (see Heb. 12:2). He has given us the Holy Spirit to guide us in our journey and to protect our faith.

True faith is not grounded in earthly things but rather has an inspired spiritual focus. We must hold fast to the truth of the gospel and to what our faith means. We must behave toward one another in the love that demonstrates our solid faith as we follow the teachings of the Bible. We must take care as to the sources of our studies into God's Word and who we follow as our Christian leaders.

> Command certain people not to teach false doctrines any longer or to devote themselves to myths and endless genealogies. Such things promote controversial speculations rather than advancing God's work—which is by faith. (1 Tim. 1:3–4; see also Eph. 4:14)

We must not let frivolous or childish, earthly desires sway or mislead us as Christians. We must not give in to the instant gratification or thrills that today's world exhibits. Our character is revealed by active, mature responses through our faith in Jesus and gospel teachings. Consider changing your atmosphere, for it fuels one's faith. This means changing your thoughts and actions, which in turn changes your consequences.

Fictional ideas concerning such things as aliens, psychic abilities, or new age mysticism are perfect examples of moving in the wrong direction. Human efforts to seek out and prove the intangible and the useless are often fraught with misinformation and danger. A true sign of Christian faith is the end result of what it produces. Fear comes from false evidence appearing true. Do not be deluded.

> Beware of false prophets, who come to you in sheep's clothing but inwardly are ravenous wolves. You will recognize them by their fruits. Are grapes gathered from thornbushes, or figs from thistles? So, every healthy tree bears good fruit, but the diseased tree bears bad fruit.

> A healthy tree cannot bear bad fruit, nor can a diseased tree bear good fruit. Every tree that does not bear good fruit is cut down and thrown into the fire. Thus you will recognize them by their fruits. (Matt. 7:15–20)

God has a plan and a purpose for everyone and everything. Trust him to help you live up to your full potential and purpose. Do not stifle these or become misdirected. Be a person of action, of purpose. The Holy Spirit equips us for a productive life with the gifts and talents we need to fulfill God's plan. True faith is demonstrated by our deeds. And those actions define all aspects of our faith and our character. One cannot have faith without deeds. Faith inspires our urge to action (see James 2:18).

> We are shown to be right with God by what we do, not by faith alone. Just as the body is dead without breath, so also faith is dead without good works. (James 2:24, 26 NLT)

THE WISDOM FOUND IN FAITH, TRUST, AND OBEDIENCE

Let God's grace work in your heart. You must trust in Jesus and let him transform your life. The more you trust, the more the mysteries of God will be revealed to you by the Holy Spirit. Wisdom and knowledge are truly hidden treasures available if we simply seek them (see Col. 2:2–3).

Belief is faith in action. Our covenant with God has an expectation of obedience in that we will be active participants in the revealing of our faith. The goal of your faith is the salvation of your soul and that of those around you. Having faith and trusting in God brings us the hope and encouragement in our lives, which we need to show and share with others. The Spirit of faith gives us the courage and strength to move through the fear and potential adversity of sharing with others the grace of God. Other people need to see our hope and to hear the reason for our hope. We are to share the hope, to give them hope (see 2 Cor. 1:3–4 NLT).

Belief strengthens our trust in coming to know God. You must believe first in order to gain the confidence to learn all you can about God. The goal is to understand the importance of becoming obedient to God. Obedience leads to successes and a productive, satisfying life. Did you know it was Jesus who said, "Anything is possible if a person believes" (see Mark 9:23 NLT)?

Faith is seen as our commitment to our trust and obedience to God. We show our faith to God by trusting in him. Obedience defines our faith and trust. We must always trust in the Lord, for he alone is the source of all life on earth and our eternity in heaven. God is forever faithful to us (see Isa. 26:4; Num. 20:12; and 2 Tim. 2:13 NLT). We see this in everything he does. It is all for us. We need to be obedient in return.

Have confidence that our faith in Jesus Christ can save us from eternal punishment for our past disobedience to God. Practice the wisdom he shares with us. Ask the Holy Spirit to guide you on the path to righteousness.

> Trust God from the bottom of your heart; don't try to figure out everything on your own. Listen for God's voice in everything you do, everywhere you go; he's the one who will keep you on track. Don't assume that you know it all. Run to God! (Prov. 3:5–7; see also 1 Cor. 1:9)

I Iave faith in your Christian beliefs and confidence in your trust of God. Trust in the knowledge that your faith will bring blessings to your life. We see evidence of this many times in the New Testament scriptures. Jesus tells one sick woman her faith has healed her (see Luke 8:40–56). Jesus encourages yet another to have no fear, merely to believe and be healed (see Luke 7:50).

Doubt is not the opposite of faith. It is struggling faith. Faith seeks understanding. We get anxious and frustrated when we don't understand something. Actively pursue answers. They are available. Everyone experiences doubts from time to time. Having other Christians in your life can help to encourage and support you in your efforts to find clarity and security. Persevere in finding the knowledge you seek. Ask for divine insight and understanding from the Holy Spirit. Trust in God to finish the good work he began in you.

> Consider it pure joy, my brothers and sisters, whenever you face trials of many kinds, because you know that the testing of your faith produces perseverance. Let perseverance finish its work so that you may be mature and complete, not lacking anything. If any of you lacks wisdom, you should ask God, who gives generously to all without finding fault, and it will be given to you. But when you ask, you must believe and not doubt, because the one who doubts is like a wave of the sea, blown and tossed by the wind. That person should not expect to receive anything from the Lord. Such a person is double-minded and unstable in all they do. (James 1:2–8)

The strength in your faith comes from trusting in God explicitly, without doubt or proof. Faith does not demand proof. Once we demand proof, it is no longer faith. There is an ever-growing confidence, which will come with the maturity of your faith. Even the disciples needed encouragement to mature in their faith. They were taught the important lesson that seeing is not the basis for believing in something. It is the confidence in your heart, where faith is borne, that will lead you to strengthening your faith and trusting in God (see John 20:29 and Rom. 10:17 NLT).

TRIALS AND SUFFERING

Why does God let bad things happen? First, let's consider the notion that God doesn't, and it's Satan tempting and attacking us. We need to take care that we don't fall prey to our own sinful desires or those of others.

> When tempted, no one should say, "God is tempting me." For God cannot be tempted by evil, nor does he tempt anyone; but each person is tempted when they are dragged away by their own evil desire and enticed. Then, after desire has conceived, it gives birth to sin; and sin, when it is full-grown, gives birth to death. (James 1:13–15)

God permits our choices—good and bad. Then we have to deal with the fallout from those decisions. We must not be self-centered, focusing on our own wants and desires. We must also avoid being led down the wrong path by the whims and fancies of others. True satisfaction does not come from any of these behaviors. Remember, you will get what you sow in your garden. Weeds or flowers? Dirt or tasty edibles (see Gal. 6:7–8 NLT)?

Always be attentive and steadfast in your convictions of right versus wrong. God has sent us his divine Spirit toward this end. So, don't hesitate to ask the Holy Spirit for help and guidance on which path to take. The Holy Spirit will often provide us with a fullness in faith and trust. For if we are filled with the right things, the less of an appetite we will have for the wrong things (see Eph. 5:18 AMP; Ps. 107:9, and Ps. 84:11).

> Be alert and of sober mind. Your enemy the devil prowls around like a roaring lion looking for someone to devour. Resist him, standing firm in the faith, because you know that the family of believers throughout the world is undergoing the same kind of sufferings. And the God of all grace, who called you to his eternal glory in Christ, after you have suffered a little while, will himself restore you and make you strong, firm and steadfast. (1 Pet. 5:8–10; see also Ps. 97:10)

Second, let's consider God's expectations concerning our outward behaviors of humility and reverence and our achieving an ultimate maturity. We have a choice to make every moment of our lives. It is time to choose to grow and mature. The testing of your faith will produce perseverance, making you mature and complete (see Job 23:10–11 and James 1:2–3). Every good thing God wants to get into your life will come from your ability to remain steadfast under trials. Guard your faith and allow yourself to grow and mature.

God seeks to make us mature and perfect, refined and complete. We must be obedient and submissive to God. He is always there for us when things get intense. Real faith comes about from our character refinement, achieved through weathering the storms of real experiences. Trials test our faith and prove its genuineness. His rewards for our persistent faith are great.

> These trials will show that your faith is genuine. It is being tested as fire tests and purifies gold—though your faith is far more precious than mere gold. So when your faith remains strong through many trials, it will bring you much praise and glory and honor on the day when Jesus Christ is revealed to the whole world. (1 Pet. 1:7 NLT)

Have confidence in your trust in God. There are no contingencies in trust. It's unconditional. God may test you to see if you are truly trusting in him. The test is for your benefit, creating a humble heart and strengthening your faith. You then can become a mature follower of Christ. Suffering can indeed produce something glorious in us. Our perseverance refines our character, and out of our character we find hope (see Rom. 5:3–4).

We know that even Jesus experienced the same fears and sufferings we do. But know this: his faith in God brought him through, and he was perfected by his trials. Even enemies of Jesus recognized his total trust in his heavenly father by the trials he endured. He demonstrated obedience to God by his perseverance. We must do the same (see Matt. 27:43 and Heb. 5:7–9).

Third, we must admit that we expect an answer to our "Why this, why me, why now?" Sometimes, things just happen. Be confident God has a plan. He will help us get through such tough times if we just ask (see Eccles. 9:12).

Jesus said, "You're asking the wrong question. You're looking for someone to blame. There is no such cause-effect here. Look instead for what God can do." (John 9:3 MSG)

We can never predict what troubles may come our way, or when they might arrive on our doorstep. Avoid the urge to run and hide, as this never accomplishes anything. We were created to participate in the human experience. The Holy Spirit will be with us and guide us through these unexpected times. God's Word teaches us how to make the most of and the best of these experiences. Do the right thing for the right reason, and leave the results to God.

Finally, trials and suffering can lead us to prayer and worship and can result in giving us renewed courage and integrity. We are never alone in our suffering. Trials have the ability to bring us closer in our relationship with God. He offers a close, responsive fellowship to those who are humble and obedient to his Word (see Isa. 66:2).

Prayer creates peace and a resting place for God's presence in your life. There is tremendous power in prayer. Pray at all times and for all things.

> Are any of you suffering hardships? You should pray. Are any of you happy? You should sing praises. Are any of you sick? You should call for the elders of the church to come and pray over you, anointing you with oil in the name of the Lord. Such a prayer offered in faith will heal the sick, and the Lord will make you well. And if you have committed any sins, you will be forgiven.
>
> Confess your sins to each other and pray for each other so that you may be healed. The earnest prayer of a righteous person has great power and produces wonderful results. (James 5:13–16 NLT)

God is not indifferent to our sufferings. He has a plan with a purpose and promises to be with us throughout all our difficult situations (see Rom. 8:28 AMP). Everything happens to achieve his purposes. We must trust him and be guided by his will. Through fire and water, God is our salvation, because we are precious and he loves us dearly. God's constant promise is to *always* be with us wherever we go (see Isa. 43:2 NLT and Josh. 1:9).

Have you ever noticed how the scriptures often use the word *through*? This means there is an entrance as well as an exit. We must never give up on God or his loving actions to help us. We must have confidence in our faith in God to respond to us at our time of need. We can get *through* anything with God's help (see 1 Cor. 10:13).

Trust in God. He created us for his glory and honor. He will never abandon us. Be brave and strong in your determination to be faithful through difficulties. God is good even when life is not. God equips us to get through difficulties. He is the source of our strength and courage (see Deut. 31:8; Isa. 41:10 NLT; and John 16:33).

There will always be the what-ifs in your life. But it is your frame of mind that will make or break you. Are you negative or positive in your attitude? It is always a burden to be focused on the negatives in life. Sometimes it feels as though we are constantly in the storms of life. My grandmother used to tell me to look for the silver lining in the clouds. She encouraged me to look for the positives—the possibilities. Learn how to change your focus and grow your faith and trust in God. We can depend on God's gift of grace and constant presence to ease our burdens. He is always with us and promises great rewards for our faithfulness, especially maintaining our faith through difficult times. Never give up!

> So we're not giving up. How could we! Even though on the outside it often looks like things are falling apart on us, on the inside, where God is making new life, not a day goes by without his unfolding grace. These hard times are

small potatoes compared to the coming good times, the lavish celebration prepared for us. There's far more here than meets the eye. The things we see now are here today, gone tomorrow. But the things we can't see now will last forever. (2 Cor. 4:16–18 MSG; see also Ps. 46:1 NLT)

God is just when we go through struggles. He comforts his people and has compassion for the afflicted. He does not forget us. He provides salvation for all who seek him out. He has great plans for us. Nothing will get in the way of those plans.

> "For I know the plans I have for you," declares the Lord, "plans to prosper you and not to harm you, plans to give you hope and a future. Then you will call on me and come and pray to me, and I will listen to you. You will seek me and find me when you seek me with all your heart." (Jer. 29:11–13; see also Matt. 6:34)

The Armory of God

God provides us with a collection of available resources for survival. Through the Holy Spirit, he provides a spiritual suit of armor to protect us as we go into battle or face tribulations. Our core strength is found in the belt of truth. The chest plate protects our heart, which holds our goodness and character. The shoes give us sure footing. A shield protects our faith. A helmet guarantees our salvation. And the sword of the Spirit is the Word of God that protects us from every evil coming our way.

> A final word: Be strong in the Lord and in his mighty power. Put on all of God's armor so that you will be able to stand firm against all strategies of the devil. For we are not fighting against flesh-and-blood enemies, but against evil rulers and authorities of the unseen world, against

mighty powers in this dark world, and against evil spirits in the heavenly places.

Therefore, put on every piece of God's armor so you will be able to resist the enemy in the time of evil. Then after the battle you will still be standing firm. Stand your ground, putting on the belt of truth and the body armor of God's righteousness. For shoes, put on the peace that comes from the Good News so that you will be fully prepared. In addition to all of these, hold up the shield of faith to stop the fiery arrows of the devil. Put on salvation as your helmet, and take the sword of the Spirit, which is the word of God.

Pray in the Spirit at all times and on every occasion. Stay alert and be persistent in your prayers for all believers everywhere. (Eph. 6:10–18 NLT)

God gives us friends—people with whom we can grow and mature. Have you ever noticed there is no back to the breastplate on a suit of armor? In Sunday school class, I was taught this is because true friends have your back. God is the best friend any of us will ever have. He will always have our backs. And he will often send our mature flesh-and-blood friends to back us up (see Eccles. 4:12 NLT and 2 Cor. 13:14).

𝓕AITH REWARDED

A life in Christ is gratifying, bringing both security and rewards. Our faith must reflect from our hearts a genuine belief and a confident trust in God. It is for others, to whom our thoughts and actions should reveal the secure reality of our faith and trust in God.

We must actively and earnestly seek God. We can always freely approach God with confidence (see Eph. 3:12). Such faith is pleasing to God. He generously and lovingly rewards those with such faith. The ultimate gratification is the reward of spending an eternity in heaven with God (see Heb. 11:6 and 1 Pet. 5:6).

> The Lord says, "I will rescue those who love me. I will protect those who trust in my name. When they call on me, I will answer; I will be with them in trouble. I will rescue and honor them. I will reward them with a long life and give them my salvation." (Ps. 91:14–16 NLT; see also 2 Sam. 7:28; Ps. 91:1–2 NLT; Ps. 37:3–6; and Heb. 10:35–36)

Be courageous and confident in what you know and believe in your heart. God will never let go. Nothing can ever strip away heavenly promises from God. He is faithful toward us. We must respond to God's promises by being faithful and obedient to his Word.

We are God's children with certain responsibilities to fulfill on our end of the covenant between us. We are called to be productive members of God's family. It is our responsibility to emulate and demonstrate righteous behavior. Our righteousness will be shown through our virtuous behavior—being without sin. Our righteousness should shine through our faithfulness and obedience to God. We have an assurance of salvation—an eternal surety. This is the ultimate reward for faithfully living a righteous life in God's Word (see 2 Pet. 1:5–8 NLT).

> For it is with your heart that you believe and are justified, and it is with your mouth that you profess your faith and are saved. As Scripture says, "Anyone who believes in him will never be put to shame." (Rom. 10:10–11; see also Phil. 3:9 and Col. 2:6–7)

In God's time, all things are revealed according to his eternal purpose. Be patient, for our rewards will come at God's designated moment (see Gal. 6:9). Eternal salvation is available to all who trust in God and place their hope and confidence in him (see Jer. 17:7–8 NLT).

Barbara L. Ayers

God's purpose is realized through Jesus and accessed through our faith in him. Believers belong to Christ. Christ dwells in our hearts through faith. Through our faith and trust in God, we become one people, working to fulfill the purpose that is the will of God.

Prayer and the Church

PRAYER IS COMMUNION. It is a genuine desire to enter into a conscious and intimate relationship with God, who is and determines the purpose of our lives. Prayer is adoration—the praise of God because of his greatness and goodness. Prayer is thanksgiving—the outpouring of gratitude to God because of his grace, mercy, and loving-kindness. Prayer is confession. It is a transparent acknowledgment of our guilty disobedience as sinful individuals. Prayer is petition, a plea for personal help. Prayer is intercession, which is defined as the petition on behalf of other people for God's intervention (see Douglas 2011).

The Word of God is how the Lord speaks to us, and prayer is how we communicate to God. Prayer is a form of speech, which reveals the power of our relationship with God. A relationship with God is a process, not an instantaneous act. It's more than just a request to change things. And it's not simply about receiving things. Prayer is about getting to know God. There is an intimacy, a closeness where we can laugh or cry and share our thoughts and feelings. Through prayer, we are free to experience life with safety, understanding, and guidance in unconditional love (see Ps. 37:4).

$\mathcal{H}$OW TO PRAY

Jesus tells his disciples how to pray, not what to pray, for that is part of the intimacy between humans and God. This personal discourse flows from deep within our hearts to be heard and responded to with unconditional love.

Most of us agree that the beginning of our prayer lives felt awkward and disjointed. Prayer takes practice and the knowledge and comfort in that there are no set rules for praying. Pray from the heart.

Jesus gave his disciples a guide to praying when they asked with great concern:

> "And when you pray, do not be like the hypocrites, for they love to pray standing in the synagogues and on the street corners to be seen by others. Truly I tell you, they have received their reward in full. But when you pray, go into your room, close the door and pray to your Father, who is unseen. Then your Father, who sees what is done in secret, will reward you. And when you pray, do not keep on babbling like pagans, for they think they will be heard because of their many words. Do not be like them, for your Father knows what you need before you ask him."

> "This, then, is how you should pray: 'Our Father in heaven, hallowed be your name, your kingdom come, your will be done, on earth as it is in heaven. Give us today our daily bread. And forgive us our debts, as we also have forgiven our debtors. And lead us not into temptation, but deliver us from the evil one.'" (Matt. 6:5–13; see also Luke 11:1–4)

Many of us like to start and end prayer with praise and worship, for praise should be given to God as an acknowledgment of and respect for his glory. After all, God is the Creator and giver of all things.

God also tells us it is best to make the time of prayer private and personal. We can feel a closeness to God when we do so. In the quiet time of our worship of him and all he is, there is a flow of comfort and empowerment filling our very being with a renewed sense of purpose.

Finally, always be authentic. God knows us and listens when we commune with him. He knows our hearts and all that concerns us. We can hide nothing from him, so don't be afraid or hesitant to share it all (see Ps. 103:1–5 and Eph. 1:11–12).

Speak with God often, as his presence is always around you. Pray at every season and event in your life. Pray for both yourself and everyone else, in good times and bad, consistently and constantly throughout your life. God gives you his best when you are at your worst. Pray out your concerns and emotional distress to God daily. Depend on God's goodness to calm your heart and strengthen you. Release it all to him (see Eph. 6:18).

Have perseverance and patience in prayer. In times of trouble and suffering, draw close to God in prayer. God hears us, and we have the assurance from Jesus that something good will come out of our pain. The Holy Spirit is with us to both comfort and intercede for us in our trying times.

> And the Holy Spirit helps us in our weakness. For example, we don't know what God wants us to pray for. But the Holy Spirit prays for us with groanings that cannot be expressed in words. And the Father who knows all hearts knows what the Spirit is saying, for the Spirit pleads for us believers in harmony with God's own will. And we know that God causes everything to work together for the good of those who love God and are called according to his purpose for them. (Rom. 8:26–28 NLT; see also 1 Cor. 3:16)

Prayer requires the right attitude and motives. We must always go to God in prayer with an attitude of humility and reverence. God knows our hearts and can see the motives behind our prayers (see James 4:3; John 14:13; and 2 Chron. 7:14). Effective prayers of a morally upright person are powerful (see James 5:16; Ps. 84:11; and James 4:8, 10).

The apostle John tells us to always pray in the name of Jesus (see John 16:23b–24). Prayer offered in the name of Jesus must be in accord with the character of Jesus. It must be presented in the same spirit of obedience and submission to God (see Heb. 5:7; Mark 14:36; and Luke 22:39–46).

The Reverend W. H. Hewitson wrote a beautiful synopsis of how prayer exists in our lives:

> There is an undercurrent of prayer that may run continually under the stream of our thoughts, and never weary us. Such prayer is the silent breathing of the Spirit of God, who dwells in our hearts (vide Rom. 8:9, and 1 Col. 3:16); it is the temper and habit of the spiritual mind; it is the pulse of our life which is hid with Christ in God. (Baillie 1886)

PRAYERS ANSWERED

God is always there. God is always hearing our voices. Of this we can be assured. God is listening even when you don't have the words. Just be in the presence of God. Just show up. Be there. He knows what is in your heart. He is aware of your needs before you even voice them (see Isa. 65:24 NLT and Isa. 30:18).

Faith is an essential component of prayer. Thanking God focuses on God's perpetual faithfulness. We must believe in God's faithfulness not only to hear but also to answer our prayers. Now, he may not answer us in ways we would think he should. But he does have a plan and answers our prayers and petitions according to those plans. There is unlimited power in the prayer of the faithful (see Matt. 21:22; Mark 11:24; James 1:5–8; and Rom. 12:12).

We need to maintain our faith in God's unceasing desire and omnipotent ability to listen to us and answer our prayers. His answer may not be what we are able to imagine within the earthly limitations of our minds. Still, it is really exciting and empowering to hear about the many ways God chooses to answer our prayers.

> Ask and it will be given to you; seek and you will find; knock and the door will be opened to you. For everyone who asks receives; the one who seeks finds; and to the one who knocks, the door will be opened.

> Which of you, if your son asks for bread, will give him a stone? Or if he asks for a fish, will give him a snake? If you, then, though you are evil, know how to give good gifts to your children, how much more will your Father in heaven give good gifts to those who ask him! (Matt. 7:7–11; see also Luke 11:9–13 NLT and Eph. 3:20 NLT)

We never have to bargain with God to have our prayers answered. Sometimes our fears are so great that we begin to promise one thing if God will grant another. This is not the way it works with God. He has a plan and a purpose yet always hears our heartfelt pleas. He is right beside us through it all. Take comfort in knowing that none of us are ever alone. God will see us through the tough times in our lives (see Ps. 34:4 NLT; Ps. 55:17; Ps. 120:1; and Ps. 139:7–8).

Why does it take so long to have prayers answered at times? Our definition of quick is not the same as God's. Human perspective does not have a heavenly equivalent. God always hears our prayers. He just responds to them as he knows best and in a time he chooses, according to his purpose. God takes the time to do everything right. Everything is done in God's time, as He wills it (see 1 John 5:14–15).

If you feel your prayer is not being answered, take time to think about your prayer. Is it in line with what God has in his plans? What motivates you in your prayer? I know many individuals who changed their specific prayer just a little bit and found it answered immediately.

We all mature in our prayer lives through time and practice. Don't feel frustrated or anxious. God does hear you. Some things just take time (see Phil. 4:6–7).

God eagerly awaits to hear from you no matter what you have to say. He wants to be an active part of your life. Thank him for what you have and ask him for what you need. There is a freedom and peace that comes from being open and honest with God.

> Come to me, all you who are weary and burdened, and I will give you rest. Take my yoke upon you and learn from me, for I am gentle and humble in heart, and you will find rest for your souls. For my yoke is easy and my burden is light. (Matt. 11:28–30)

PRAYER AND THE CHURCH

Pray together. There is power in prayer and even more power in greater numbers. Think of it like a hanging chandelier. One lightbulb is okay. But as you add more and more, the light gets brighter and brighter. We can accomplish so much more if we pray and worship together (see Matt. 18:19–20; Eph. 5:19–20; and Col. 3:16).

United in faith, Christians make up the family of God and are often referred to as the church. We become one flesh, one body, with one purpose. We have been given clear instructions concerning our worship practices as his people, the church of Christ. There is an expectation, an obligation to follow God's Word in worship and prayer. Prayer empowers us as a people. We receive courage, strength, and peace through all our prayers in the Spirit of Christ (see Phil. 4:13 AMP; 1 Cor. 14:33; Eph. 3:10–11; and 1 Tim. 2:1–2).

*E*DIFICATION OF THE CHURCH BODY

We are not just a culture of belonging. We were created to be social and to have relationships. People need relationships to learn and be nurtured. They help to keep us knowledgeable and accountable. We require social interactions to give us a sense of fulfillment in life. Isolation brings emptiness. More importantly, there is nothing as wonderful as being among positive, supportive people to make us positive and supportive in return.

We need other Christians to help us deal with things we encounter in this earthly life. We do not and should not exist in isolation. We need others to support and strengthen our spiritual growth. There is tremendous power in our Christian relationships. Just as Jesus leads us in love to places that we need to be, he will lead us to people who will help us to grow and mature.

> Just as a body, though one, has many parts, but all its many parts form one body, so it is with Christ. For we were all baptized by one Spirit so as to form one body— whether Jews or Gentiles, slave or free—and we were all given the one Spirit to drink. Even so the body is not made up of one part but of many.
>
> There should be no division in the body, but that its parts should have equal concern for each other. If one part suffers, every part suffers with it; if one part is honored, every part rejoices with it.
>
> Now you are the body of Christ, and each one of you is a part of it. (1 Cor. 12:12–14, 25–27; see also Eph. 4:16 and Rom 12:4–5)

We all require the church body for edification, for moral and intellectual instruction and improvement. We are responsible for teaching others and for continuing to learn ourselves. We must set good examples of just and proper everyday living. We must always be available to help one another to maintain a focus on behaving morally upright, without guilt or sin. Guidance and service cannot be limited to Sundays and religious holidays. We need frequent contact with the church body. It should be treated like the important part of our lives that it is. Just as the human body cannot live or function well without its parts, so does a church require all its members. A missing piece is deeply felt by all.

We receive spiritual gifts from the Holy Spirit to mature the church body and to serve one another. Each one of us receives the gift of a talent, which is uniquely designed specifically for that person. Each member uses their own talent(s) to perform their own work and so contribute to the whole. It is each person exercising his or her own gift within the whole body that produces spiritual growth in both the giver and the receiver (see 1 Cor. 12:4–6, 11; Eph. 4:12–13; and 1 Pet. 4:10).

Many of us are inexperienced or lacking in a complete knowledge in the doctrine of righteousness—of conforming to the divine will in purpose, thought, and action. We must seek out trained and worthy leaders and study groups to help teach, guide, and walk alongside us. This is crucial to our development as Christians. Surrounding ourselves with other like-minded people is the best way to survive this life on earth. An important role of the church is to provide support until we return home to our heavenly Father.

An enormous benefit of belonging to a church is that our thinking and behavior are kept in check. It allows us to practice and perfect appropriate thoughts and behaviors so they become a natural part of our very being—a habit per se. The company with whom we keep rubs off on us.

Sometimes we need to take a season away from old friends and acquaintances to give ourselves time to grow and mature. Old friends may get in the way of our work in developing and changing our attitudes and behaviors. We need time to practice who we desire to be. Bad company corrupts good behavior. Separation might give us a greater chance of becoming that person of whom we can be proud—the person we were always meant to become.

Along with supporting and building up one another, we are also called upon to discipline or correct one another. This must always come from a place of love and not punishment. A mature Christian can give admonishment in a guiding way, without being hurtful. Alas, we need to be both willing to give *and* to accept wise counsel from knowledgeable Christians. Do both with grace and humility (see Prov. 15:31–32 and Prov. 12:1).

We must always discern between sound discipline and personal judgment before we act. We are not to pass judgment on one another. Such action comes not from a loving heart but a jealous mind. One must take care not to execute a person while executing guidance. We must be a safe place for others. Soften your ways to act with self-control, respect, and, most importantly, love (see Matt. 7:1–2; Rom. 14:10–12; and Gal. 6:1 NLT).

Yes, we all have good days and bad days. And along with our fellow Christians, at any time of day or night, we are expected to lift up and support those who are in need, both physically and spiritually. We must be available with the right attitudes and motives. We already know that attitudes and actions are contagious. Our best work will be completed and appreciated when we carry a healthy attitude in our demeanor.

We must always be prepared to build up one another in all circumstances with the same unconditional love God shows us. "We can do all things through God's will. And where there's a good will, there's always a good way to get things done." This is what my mother always assured me (see Eph. 4:25–29 and Eph. 4:2).

> Those of us who are strong and able in the faith need to step in and lend a hand to those who falter, and not just do what is most convenient for us. Strength is for service,

not status. Each one of us needs to look after the good of
the people around us, asking ourselves, "How can I help?"
(Rom. 15:1–2 MSG)

Christians are not perfect people. We are all equal in our sins and
must work continually to meet the expectations of God (see Rom. 3:23).
If anyone were perfect, we never would have required God to step in
and sacrifice his Son for our salvation. We cannot be good enough, earn
enough, or become deserving enough to gain salvation. It is a free gift, paid
for with the sacrifice of Jesus Christ. We have to want it and accept it. Then
God will restore us to the best version of who he made us to be. We are
expected to emulate Christlike behavior and do the same for others—to
help each one of them to become the best version of themselves.

We have such an incredible need for each of us to become mature
Christians. Together we must help one another to accomplish this. We
need to unite so we can grow and survive both physically and spiritually.
We exist as one, in unity. We are a family, the children of God. Our
church family acts as a compass to keep us on course, headed in the right
direction—physically, intellectually, morally, and spiritually. The family
members keep us grounded and focused. We need one another immensely
(see Eccles. 4:10 and Prov. 27:17).

Therefore encourage one another and build each other up,
just as in fact you are doing.

Now we ask you, brothers and sisters, to acknowledge those
who work hard among you, who care for you in the Lord
and who admonish you. Hold them in the highest regard
in love because of their work. Live in peace with each
other. And we urge you, brothers and sisters, warn those
who are idle and disruptive, encourage the disheartened,
help the weak, be patient with everyone. Make sure that
nobody pays back wrong for wrong, but always strive to
do what is good for each other and for everyone else.

Rejoice always, pray continually, give thanks in all circumstances; for this is God's will for you in Christ Jesus. (1 Thess. 5:11–18; see also Heb. 10:24–25; Rom. 15:5–7; and Phil. 2:3–4 NLT)

$\mathcal{A}$MBASSADORS OF CHRIST IN RECONCILIATION AND SALVATION

There is a strength and confidence in being a Christian. There is also a peace that fills our hearts and enables us to do most anything. We are charged with the greatest task—watching over one another in righteousness and love (see Acts 20:28; Isa. 1:16–17; and 2 Pet. 3:10–11).

Be ready. Be good servants. Actively serve God and one another. Use God's principles for living life. Be good examples of righteousness—living a morally right and justifiable life. Never pass up an opportunity to answer somebody as to why you live the way you do.

> If with heart and soul you're doing good, do you think you can be stopped? Even if you suffer for it, you're still better off. Don't give the opposition a second thought. Through thick and thin, keep your hearts at attention, in adoration before Christ, your Master. Be ready to speak up and tell anyone who asks why you're living the way you are, and always with the utmost courtesy. Keep a clear conscience before God so that when people throw mud at you, none of it will stick. They'll end up realizing that *they're* the ones who need a bath. It's better to suffer for doing good, if that's what God wants, than to be punished for doing bad. That's what Christ did definitively: suffered because of others' sins, the Righteous One for the unrighteous ones. He went through it all—was put to death and then made alive—to bring us to God. (1 Pet. 3:15–18 MSG; see also Matt. 5:16; 2 Cor. 5:18–21; and Col. 4:5–6)

CONCLUSION IN BREVI

Join together with like-minded people to become the person God has always planned for you to be. Together we can make it through the darkness of this world into the light God has promised to us. There will be a day in the not too distant future when all the mysteries of God will be revealed. I know I want to be there for this awesome time. You will definitely want to be a participant in the new life Jesus has described and promised to us.

Time is of the essence. The Lord will return as he promised. He will gather together all who trust and emulate him. They will join him in a personal relationship with God for an eternity in heaven. Nobody knows when this new life will occur, so isn't it better to always be alert and prepared? Tempus fugit.

> But about that day or hour no one knows, not even the angels in heaven, nor the Son, but only the Father. As it was in the days of Noah, so it will be at the coming of the Son of Man. For in the days before the flood, people were eating and drinking, marrying and giving in marriage, up to the day Noah entered the ark; and they knew nothing about what would happen until the flood came and took them all away. That is how it will be at the coming of the Son of Man. Two men will be in the field; one will be taken and the other left. Two women will be grinding with a hand mill; one will be taken and the other left.
>
> Therefore keep watch, because you do not know on what day your Lord will come. But understand this: If the owner of the house had known at what time of night the thief was coming, he would have kept watch and would not have let his house be broken into. So you also must be ready, because the Son of Man will come at an hour when you do not expect him. (Matt. 24:36–44; see also Mark 13:32–37 and Luke 12:40)

Quotes and References by Chapter Heading In Biblical Order

A Defining Moment

Quotes

Proverbs 15:21–24
   (MSG)
Proverbs 19:20–21
Jeremiah 33:3 (MSG)
Romans 1:20
Ephesians 1:9–10
Ephesians 4:1–6
1 Peter 3:15

References

Micah 6:8 (MSG)
Colossians 4:5–6 (NLT)

God

Quotes

Ecclesiastes 3:11–14
Isaiah 55:8–9
Jeremiah 33:2–3
John 5:24–25
Romans 1:20 (NLT)
Hebrews 6:16–19 (NLT)
Revelation 21:5–8 (NLT)
Merriam-Webster. com Dictionary, s.v. "holy," accessed June 6, 2020, https://www. merriam–webster.com/ dictionary/holy.

References

Genesis 1:26; 3:22; 11:7
Genesis 18:1–14; 17:17
Exodus 3:14–15
Exodus 20:3 (NLT)
Exodus 20:5
Exodus 34:6–7
Exodus 34:14
Numbers 23:19
Deuteronomy 4:24; 5:9; 6:15; 32:16; 32:21
Deuteronomy 7:9–10 (NLT)
Deuteronomy 30:19–20
Joshua 24:19
1 Chronicles 29:11
Job 11:7–8
Job 42:2
Psalm 18

Psalm 19:1–4
Psalm 37:4
Psalm 90:2, 4
Psalm 130:3 (NLT)
Psalm 139:1–6 (AMP)
Psalm 139:7–10
Proverbs 3:11–12
Proverbs 16:9
Isaiah 6:8a
Isaiah 30:18 (MSG)
Isaiah 40:28 (MSG)
Isaiah 43:1–4 (MSG)
Isaiah 43:7
Isaiah 43:10b
Isaiah 43:11a (MSG)
Isaiah 43:25 (MSG)
Isaiah 45:22–23a (NLT)
Isaiah 44:6–8 (MSG)
Isaiah 46:9
Isaiah 48:17
Isaiah 65:1
Jeremiah 23:24
Jeremiah 29:13
Ezekiel 36:5–6; 39:25
Amos 4:13
Nahum 1:2
Matthew 6:33
Matthew 13:3b–9 (NLT)
Matthew 15:1–6 (NLT)
Matthew 19:26b
Matthew 28:19
Mark 4:14–20 (MSG)
Luke 1:5–25
Luke 8:4–15 (NLT)
Luke 12:36
John 1:12–13

John 4:24
John 6:29
John 7:16–17
John 11:1–45
John 12:38–40 (NLT)
Acts 17:26 (NLT)
Acts 17:27 (NLT)
Romans 9:16–23 (NLT)
1 Corinthians 2:7
1 Corinthians 8:6a
Ephesians 1:4–6
Ephesians 3:14–17
Ephesians 4:6
1 Timothy 2:1–4
2 Timothy 1:9
Hebrews 2:1–3 (NLT)
Hebrews 12:5–7a, 10b–11
James 1:17
1 Peter 1:1–2
2 Peter 3:8
Revelation 1:8
Revelation 3:20a
Revelation 22:13

Jesus Christ

Quotes

Isaiah 42:1–4, 6–7, 9
Isaiah 53:1–12
John 3:16–18
John 5:24–30
Colossians 1:15–23
1 John 4:9–10, 14b–16
St. Augustine of Hippo,
  AD 354–430
Douglas, J. D.,
  Merrill C.
Tenney, and Silva
Moisés. Zondervan
Illustrated Bible
Dictionary. Grand
Rapids, MI:
Zondervan,
2011. 268, 734.

References

Psalm 22:1–31
Psalm 118:22
Isaiah 7:13–16
Isaiah 9:6–7
Isaiah 11:1–5, 10–11
Isaiah 28:16–18
Isaiah 53:3
Jeremiah 23:5
Jeremiah 31:31–34
Micah 5:2–4
Zechariah 9:9–10
Matthew 1:1–17
Matthew 1:18–23
Matthew 18:12–14
  (NLT)

Matthew 20:17–19
Matthew 21:42–44
Mark 8:31–33
Mark 9:30–32
Mark 10:32–33
Luke 1:26–35
Luke 1:68–70
Luke 13:31–33
Luke 15:3–7
Luke 18:31–33
Luke 19:10
Luke 24:13–51
Luke 24:44
John 1:1–3, 14
John 1:4–5,
John 1:9
John 1:10–13
John 1:18 (NLT)
John 1:29, 36
John 2:16–22
John 3:19–21
John 6:35, 41, 48, 51
John 8:12
John 8:23
John 8:58
John 9:5
John 10:7–14
John 10:11, 14–15
John 10:17–18
John 10:28–30 (AMP)
John 11:25–26
John 12:37–41
John 12:42–43
John 13:13
John 14:6–7
John 14:9–10

John 14:12
John 14:19–20
John 15:1–5
John 15:25 (NLT)
John 17:17
John 18:37
John 19:28–30
Acts 1:3, 9–11
Acts 4:12
Acts 10:38
Acts 10:39–43
Romans 3:25
Romans 4:25
Romans 5:8–11
Romans 8:1–2
1 Corinthians 8:6
1 Corinthians 15:3–4
1 Corinthians 15:3–8
1 Corinthians 15:20–22
2 Corinthians 4:6
2 Corinthians 5:18–20
2 Corinthians 5:21
Galatians 3:28
Galatians 4:4–6
Ephesians 2:14–18,
  19–22
Philippians 2:6–8
Colossians 1:16
1 Timothy 2:5–6 (NLT)
Hebrews 1:3
Hebrews 2:14
Hebrews 4:15
1 Peter 1:18–2
1 John 1:7

Holy Spirit

Quotes

Isaiah 30:21
Ezekiel 36:26–27
Matthew 3:16
Matthew 12:31–32
Romans 8:1–17
1 Corinthians 2:9–16
1 Corinthians 12:4–11
Galatians 5:22–23, 25
1 John 4:12–15

Romans 15:13
1 Corinthians 2:7
1 Corinthians 6:19–20
1 Corinthians 12:3
2 Corinthians 3:13–18
2 Corinthians 13:14
Ephesians 1:17
Ephesians 4:30
1 Thessalonians 1:5
2 Timothy 1:7
2 Timothy 1:14
Hebrews 10:29
Hebrews 6:4–6
James 1:5
2 Peter 1:20–21

References

Genesis 1:1–2 (NLT)
Exodus 31:3
Job 26:13 (NLT)
Psalm 33:6
Proverbs 9:10
Joel 2:28–29
Matthew 10:19–20
Luke 11:13
Luke 12:11–12
John 3:3–12
John 3:34
John 14:16–17
John 14:25–26
John 15:26 (NLT)
John 16:13–15
Acts 1:8
Acts 2:38
Acts 4:31
Acts 5:1–10
Acts 10:44
Acts 15:8
Romans 5:5
Romans 8:26–27

Scripture and Disciples

Quotes

Psalm 78:1–7
Proverbs 1:2–7
Proverbs 3:5–7 (MSG)
Isaiah 30:8–11 (MSG)
Matthew 7:15–19 (MSG)
Matthew 13:10–17 (MSG)
Mark 16:19–20
John 14:1–3
John 15:5, 7–8
Romans 16:25–26 (MSG)
Ephesians 3:1–13 (MSG)
2 Timothy 3:16–17

Isaiah 6:8–13 (NLT)
Isaiah 48:17
Jeremiah 15:16 (NLT)
Matthew 4:4 (MSG)
Matthew 5:10–12
Matthew 10:1–8
Matthew 28:16–20
Mark 4:10–20, 33–34 (MSG)
Mark 8:34
Luke 8:10–15 (MSG)
Luke 9:23–24
Luke 10:3
Luke 11:49
John 3:12
John 8:31–32
John 13:34–35
John 15:15
John 20:19–22
John 20:30
John 21:25
Acts 3:1–10, 16
Acts 6:8
Acts 8:6–7
Acts 9:17–18
Acts 9:33–41
Acts 14:8–10
Acts 15:12
Acts 16:16–19
Acts 19:11–12
Acts 20:9–12
Acts 28:7–9
Romans 6:17 (MSG)
Romans 12:18
Romans 15:4 (NLT)

1 Corinthians 10:11 (NLT)
1 Corinthians 2:7
2 Corinthians 4:2–4
2 Corinthians 5:19–20
Colossians 1:26–27
Ephesian 1:9 (NLT)
Ephesians 6:4
Philippians 2:2–5
1 Thessalonians 4:18 (NLT)
2 Timothy 3:15
Hebrews 4:12
Hebrews 12:1–11 (MSG)
Hebrews 13:8–9
James 1:22–25
1 Peter 1:22–25 (MSG)
2 Peter 1:19–21
1 John 4:1

References

Leviticus 19:31
Leviticus 20:6
Deuteronomy 18:10–12
Joshua 1:8 (NLT)
1 Chronicles 10:13–14 (MSG)
Job 12:25
Psalm 33:4–6
Psalm 119:89–96 (MSG)
Psalm 119:114 (MSG)
Psalm 119:124–128 (MSG)
Psalm 119:129–136 (MSG)
Proverbs 3:27
Proverbs 5:1–2
Proverbs 15:10
Isaiah 42:20 (NLT)

Covenants and Commandments

Quotes

Psalm 1:1–3
Psalm 119:169–176
  (NLT)
Ecclesiastes 12:13–14
Jeremiah 31:31–34
  (NLT)
Matthew 22:37–40
Romans 7:7–11
Hebrews 6:16–19 (NLT)
Hebrews 8:6–13

Romans 7:4–6 (NLT)
Romans 8:1–2
Romans 13:9–10 (NLT)
1 Corinthians 11:25
1 Corinthians 15:51–57
  (NLT)
2 Corinthians 3:6
2 Corinthians 5:17
Galatians 2:16
Galatians 2:19–21
Galatians 4:4–5
Galatians 5:4–6
Galatians 6:13–15
Ephesians 6:7
Ephesians 2:14–15
  (NLT)
Philippians 3:8–9
Colossians 2:13–15
Colossians 2:20–23
Hebrews 10:28
James 2:10
2 Peter 3:9 (NLT)
2 Peter 3:15

References

Genesis 4:21
Genesis 6–9
Genesis 12:3; 17:7; 17:13
Genesis 12, 15, 17
2 Samuel 7:16
Psalm 25:14 (NLT)
Psalm 103:17–18 (NLT)
Psalm 119:33–34
Psalm 119:93 (NLT)
Proverbs 14:22
Micah 6:8
Matthew 7:12
Matthew 15:6
Mark 10:45 (NLT)
Mark 14:24 (NLT)
Luke 10:25–27
John 1:17
John 13:34
Acts 13:38–39
Romans 3:20
Romans 4:13–16
Romans 6:15–23

Earthly versus Heavenly Focus

Quotes

Romans 8:32

2 Corinthians 4:16–18
(MSG)

2 Corinthians 5:14–20
(MSG)

Ephesians 2:1–5 (MSG)

Ephesians 4:21–24
(NLT)

Ephesians 5:1–5

Philippians 3:17–21

1 Timothy 6:6–10,
17–19 (NLT)

James 3:13–18

References

1 Samuel 16:7

Job 28 NLT

Psalm 73:1–28 (MSG)

Psalm 111:10

Proverbs 1:7

Proverbs 2:1–11

Proverbs 4:23

Proverbs 27:19

Proverbs 29:25 (MSG)

Ecclesiastes 5:19 (NLT)

Jeremiah 17:5–8

Ezekiel 36:26

Matthew 6:19–21; 24–33
(NLT)

Mark 13:31

Luke 11:17

Luke 12:15

Luke 12:21

Luke 12:23–31

Luke 12:34

Luke 12:24–28 (NLT)

Luke 16:13

Luke 16:15

Luke 16:19–29

Luke 21:1–4

Luke 21:34–36

John 6:35

Acts 17:26–27

Romans 8:29 (AMP)

Romans 12:2 (NLT)

Romans 13:11–14

1 Corinthians 3:16

1 Corinthians 6:18–20

2 Corinthians 1:12

2 Corinthians 7:1

Galatians 5:16–21

Galatians 5:24

Galatians 6:7–8

Ephesians 4:17–19

Ephesians 5:17–18

Philippians 4:8

Colossians 3:1–2 (NLT)

Colossians 3:12–14

2 Timothy 4:3–4

Titus 2:12 (NLT)

1 Peter 1:14

2 Peter 1:4 (NLT)

2 Peter 3:10–13

1 John 2:15–16

Grace and Salvation

Quotes

Isaiah 62:11 (NLT)
Romans 5:16
Romans 6:11–14
Ephesians 2:8–9 (NLT)
1 Timothy 2:4–7 (MSG)
2 Timothy 1:9–10

References

Genesis 3
Psalm 40:8
Psalm 91:14–16
Isaiah 12:2
Isaiah 30:19 (MSG)
Isaiah 65:17–25
Jeremiah 33:14–16
    (NLT)
Matthew 5:16 (NLT)
Matthew 11:28
Luke 1:76–78
Luke 12:48b
John 1:17
Acts 2:21
Acts 15:11
Romans 3:21–25
Romans 5:12–19
Acts 4:12
Romans 3:28
Romans 6:23
Romans 8:1
Romans 10:9, 13
Romans 11:6
Romans 11:11 (NLT)
Romans 11:35–36
1 Corinthians 1:18

1 Corinthians 15:9 10
2 Corinthians 1:12
2 Corinthians 5:10
2 Corinthians 7:10
Galatians 5:4
Ephesians 1:6–7 (NLT)
Ephesians 1:13–14
Ephesians 4:7
Philippians 2:12–13
    (NLT)
Titus 2:11–12
Titus 3:4–7
Hebrews 2:3–4
Hebrews 4:16
James 5:11
1 Peter 1:13
2 Peter 3:8–9 (NLT)
2 Peter 3:10–11, 13

Forgiveness and Love

Quotes

Matthew 9:12–13
Matthew 12:31–32
  (MSG)
Romans 7:17–25 (MSG)
1 Corinthians 13:1–7
  (MSG)
1 Corinthians 13:12–13
  (MSG)
Philippians 2:1–4
Colossians 3:12–14
1 John 4:7–12, 16–19
1 John 4:18

References

Deuteronomy 6:4–5
Leviticus 19:18
Psalm 33:4–5
Psalm 32:1–2
Psalm 86:5
Psalm 103:8–12
Psalm 107:43
Psalm 130:1–8
Psalm 136:1, 26
Proverbs 11:25
Proverbs 21:21
Isaiah 43:16, 18–19
Isaiah 54:10
Jeremiah 31:3 (AMP)
Jeremiah 33:11
Ezekiel 18:21–22 (NLT)
Matthew 3:8
Matthew 5:24
Matthew 6:14–15
Matthew 10:8

Matthew 22:37–40
Mark 3:28–29
Mark 12:28–31 (NLT)
Luke 6:37
Luke 10:25–27
Luke 12:8–10
John 3:16
John 13:34
John 14:21 (NLT)
John 15:12
John 15:13
Acts 10:43
Romans 5:8
Romans 8:28
Romans 8:37–39
Romans 12:9–10
Romans 13:8–10
1 Corinthians 2:9
1 Corinthians 16:13–14
Galatians 5:13–14
Ephesians 1:7
Ephesians 3:17–19
Ephesians 4:32
Ephesians 5:1–2
Philippians 1:9–10
1 Timothy 1:5
Hebrews 9:22
1 Peter 1:22
1 John 1:8–9
1 John 3:11
1 John 3:16
1 John 3:18
1 John 4:20–21
Zavada, Jack. "Agape:
  What Does the Bible
  Say About the Highest

Form of Love?" *Learn
Religions. Learn
Religions,* April 17,
2019. https://www.
learnreligions.com/
agape-love-in-the-
bible-700675.

Faith and Trust

Quotes

Psalm 91:14–16 (NLT)
Proverbs 3:5–7
Jeremiah 29:11–13
Matthew 7:15–20
Mark 9:23 NLT
John 9:3 MSG
Romans 10:10–11
2 Corinthians 4:16–18
   (MSG)
Ephesians 6:10–18
   (NLT)
1 Timothy 1:3–4
Hebrews 11:1–2,
James 1:2–8
James 1:13–15
James 2:24, 26 (NLT)
James 5:13–16 (NLT)
1 Peter 1:7 (NLT)
1 Peter 5:8–10

Ecclesiastes 9:12 (NLT)
Isaiah 26:4
Isaiah 41:10 (NLT)
Isaiah 43:2 (NLT)
Isaiah 66:2
Jeremiah 17:7–8 (NLT)
Matthew 6:34
Matthew 8:23–26
Matthew 27:43
Mark 4:35–40
Luke 7:50
Luke 8:40–56
John 16:33 (NLT)
John 20:29
Romans 4:18–21
Romans 5:1–2
Romans 5:3–4
Romans 8:28 (AMP)
Romans 10:17 (NLT)
Romans 15:13 (NLT)
1 Corinthians 1:9
1 Corinthians 10:13
2 Corinthians 1:3–4
   (NLT)
2 Corinthians 5:7
2 Corinthians 13:14
Galatians 6:7–8 (NLT)
Galatians 6:9
Ephesians 5:18 (AMP)
Ephesians 3:12
Ephesians 4:14
Philippians 3:9
Colossians 2:2–3
Colossians 2:6–7
2 Timothy 2:13 (NLT)
Hebrews 5:7–9

Hebrews 10:35–36
Hebrews 11:6
Hebrews 11:13–16
Hebrew 11:39–40
Hebrews 12:2
James 1:2–3
James 2:18
1 Peter 5:6
2 Peter 1:5–8 (NLT)

References

Genesis 17:17
Numbers 20:12
Deuteronomy 31:8
Joshua 1:9
2 Samuel 7:28
Job 23:10–11
Psalm 37:3–6
Psalm 46:1 (NLT)
Psalm 84:11
Psalm 91:1–2 (NLT)
Psalm 97:10
Psalm 107:9
Ecclesiastes 4:12 (NLT)

Prayer and the Church

Quotes

Matthew 6:5–13
Matthew 7:7–11
Matthew 11:28–30
Matthew 24: 36–42
Romans 8:26–28 (NLT)
Romans 15:1–2 (MSG)
1 Corinthians 12:12–14,
  25–27
1 Thessalonians 5:11–18
1 Peter 3:15–18 (MSG)
Baillie, Rev. John.
  Memoir of the Rev.
W. H. Hewitson. London:
  James
Nisbet, 1886. 100–101.

References

2 Chronicles 7:14
Psalm 34:4
Psalm 37:4
Psalm 55:17
Psalm 84:11
Psalm 103:1–5
Psalm 120:1
Psalm 139:7–8
Proverbs 12:1
Proverbs 15:31–32
Proverbs 27:17
Ecclesiastes 4:10
Isaiah 1:16–17
Isaiah 30:18
Isaiah 65:24 (NLT)
Matthew 5:16
Matthew 7:1–2

Matthew 18:19–20
Matthew 21:22
Mark 11:24
Mark 13:32–37
Mark 14:36
Luke 11:1–4
Luke 11:9–13 (NLT)
Luke 12:40
Luke 22:39–46
John 14:13
John 16:23b–24
Acts 20:28
Romans 3:23
Romans 12:4–5
Romans 12:12
Romans 14:10–12
Romans 15:5–7
1 Corinthians 3:16
1 Corinthians 12:4–6, 11
1 Corinthians 14:33
2 Corinthians 5:18–21
Galatians 6:1 (NLT)
Ephesians 1:11 12
Ephesians 3:10–11
Ephesians 3:20 (NLT)
Ephesians 4:2
Ephesians 4:12–13
Ephesians 4:16
Ephesians 4:25–29
Ephesians 5:19–20
Ephesians 6:18
Philippians 2:3–4 (NLT)
Philippians 4:6–7
Philippians 4:13 (AMP)
Colossians 3:16
Colossians 4:5–6

1 Timothy 2:1–2
Hebrews 5:7
Hebrews 10:24–25
James 1:5–8
James 4:3
James 4:8, 10
James 5:16
1 Peter 4:10
2 Peter 3:10–11
1 John 5:14–15
Douglas, J. D.,
  Merrill C. Tenney,
  and Silva Moisés.
  *Zondervan Illustrated
  Bible Dictionary.*
  Grand Rapids, MI:
  Zondervan, 2011.
  1165–1167.

About the Author

BARBARA HOLDS UNDERGRADUATE degrees in psychology and anthropology, a master's in counseling, and a degree in paralegal studies. She is a nationally certified counselor and currently resides in southern Arizona.

Barbara is the author of *Always Protect Your Behind: A Life Guide for Young Adults or Misguided Old Ones*, published in August 2014 by Telemachus Press, available in e-book or paperback from your favorite bookseller.

Defining Christianity: In Brevi began as a research project to help the author explain her Christian faith to her family and friends. This book is the resulting manuscript she has decided to share with everyone. It is her sincere hope and prayer that it has a profound impact on someone's life.

As the disciple Paul said, "And this is my prayer: that your love may abound more and more in knowledge and depth of insight, so that you may be able to discern what is best and may be pure and blameless for the day of Christ, filled with the fruit of righteousness that comes through Jesus Christ—to the glory and praise of God" (Philippians 1:9–11 NIV).

Printed in the United States
By Bookmasters